The Drive

in '65

An epic road trip, a journey of discovery

Sandra Lynne Reed

Paperback: ISBN 978-1-7350376-0-8

E-book: ISBN 978-1-7350376-1-5

Editing and interior design by Julie McDonald Zander
Cover design by Jenny Q of Historical Fiction Book Covers
Cover photograph from the author's personal collection

Paperback sold in the U.S.A. are also printed in the U.S.A.

Published by Parenti Publishing
P.O. Box 104, Sequim, WA 98382

Visit www.SandraLynneReed.com

Dedication

Dedicated to Winnie and Phyllis.
Without their adventuresome spirits,
many of my own life's adventures
would never have taken place.

PHYLLIS (SANDERS)
(CLARK) MASON
1927-2013

WINNIE (SANDERS)
(REED) PERMAN
1934-2017

Acknowledgments

While much of book-writing is a solitary affair, people other than the author participate in vital ways. My siblings Marlie and Glenn answered many questions about the adventure we enjoyed together, and even Dyana, born after our return from the Drive in '65, contributed because she knows much of the story by heart.

Other family members, including my uncle Don Sanders and cousin Suzan Frank, shared their memories, and many of my cousins among the Sanders Clan and Affiliated Members (SCAM) have cheered my progress.

Few writers reach the point of publication without a community of other writers contributing their critiques, early readings, and the benefit of their own experience. Among these, Lisa Preston, Eva Stanfield, and Laura Vosika responded very helpfully to early reads. Many others cheered me along through early critiques and later revisions. Julie McDonald Zander provided personal encouragement along with her professional expertise.

And of course, my husband, Vern, made room in his life for this book, too, and he gave me an office of my own. His support and tolerance for my writing pursuits bring joy and thankfulness for our life together. Our children, Vienna, Marina, and Mark, have each found personal ways to encourage me.

Contents

Chapter 1 7
Chapter 2 20
Chapter 3 30
Chapter 4 41
Chapter 5 49
Chapter 6 57
Chapter 7 63
Chapter 8 72
Chapter 9 78
Chapter 10 90
Chapter 11 97
Chapter 12 103
Chapter 13 109
Chapter 14 118
Chapter 15 129
Chapter 16 136
Chapter 17 147
Chapter 18 153
Chapter 19 161
Chapter 20 171
Chapter 21 181
Chapter 22 187
Chapter 23 191
Chapter 24 198
Chapter 25 209
Chapter 26 215
Chapter 27 223
Author's Note...232

Chapter 1

MARLIE AND GLENN and I tickled and teased in the back seat as Dad drove our '57 Chevy south along Turnagain Arm. We passed frozen waterfalls on the left, and the sharp drop to the edge of the water on the right, with almost no shoulders and not near enough guardrails. We drove the hundred-mile stretch from Anchorage to Moose Pass thirty or forty weekends a year, but this time we stayed for ten days, clear through Christmas and into the new year, 1963.

An hour from Anchorage, we veered away from the water. The road climbed through the white country, as we called Turnagain Pass, and past the mountains where Dad hunted sheep in the fall. Snowbanks rose higher than the car windows through that alpine territory. As we youngsters started bouncing on the back seat, Mom said, "Come on, kids, let's sing a song."

"The Sloop John B!" I called out.

"Okay, you other kids can choose next." She burst into song, quieting our rambunctious behavior without us even knowing it. By the time we reached Moose Pass, we'd gone through some Jim Reeves, folk songs, and a few popular numbers that we knew Mom's brothers would sing when we saw them for Christmas, playing their guitars at Aunt Phyllis's house.

We knew everybody who lived in every house in Moose Pass, about a hundred people in the townsite, and a few more in isolated cabins along the highway to the north and south. Our family had lived there until 1957.

My family celebrated Christmas of 1962 as we usually did, gathered at Aunt Phyllis's house in Moose Pass. Most of my twenty cousins were in town for the holiday. We kids were sent upstairs or shushed long enough for the family's annual splurge on a phone call to their youngest sister, Aunt Betty. She'd married and moved to Virginia a few years earlier.

One afternoon Mom and Aunt Phyllis began to reminisce.

"Wouldn't it be great to just show up at Betty's door one day?" Mom imagined Betty's shock.

"I'd love that!" Phyllis sipped her coffee. "And how about our cousins on Long Island? It would be great to surprise them, ring the doorbell and wait to see the looks on their faces."

Mom's parents brought their seven kids from Smithtown, New York, to Moose Pass, Alaska, in 1945, and most of them still lived in Alaska in the 1960s. Back on Long Island, Mom and her six siblings had been surrounded by cousins who became their closest childhood friends. Now the same thing happened with their family in Alaska—all Mom's siblings had children. During the 1950s

8

alone, seventeen grandchildren were born to Gram and Grampa Sanders.

One of the kids, running through the kitchen, stopped to ask, "Who should we meet?"

"Aunt Betty, and our relatives in New York."

Virginia and New York, so far from our small world, might as well have been the moon. Born and raised in the land of the midnight sun, the rest of the country hovered in the distance, beyond our reach, or even our imagination. Beyond the hundred miles of highway between Moose Pass and Anchorage. On rare occasions we explored more widely, clam digging or agate hunting along the shores of Cook Inlet, or watching the Mount Marathon race in Seward on the Fourth of July. Moose and mountain goats inhabited our world. We had never seen a herd of cows.

Mom's eyes sparkled, her mind churning. "It would be a really long trip, but..."

Phyllis liked to dream big. "If we go that far, we might as well see all the people and places we can."

"Yeah! If we drove to New York and Virginia, we could go a little farther and visit Uncle Sal and Uncle Nick in Florida." Grandma perked up hearing that. She hadn't seen her brothers in years.

Soon the list included natural wonders and historic buildings, amusements and amazements of all kinds. We kids chimed in with our own desires: Niagara Falls! The Grand Canyon! Disneyland!

The extravagance might have sunk the plan. After all, Mom and Phyllis grew up poor, sometimes living in a relative's garage where rats bit their sister Nancy one night. But they had learned to economize, growing gardens and serving Spam roasts studded with cloves when they had no more salmon or moose meat in the freezer. With their kids all in school, both of them worked at paying jobs.

Maybe, just maybe, they could make it happen.

We chattered about the trip all the way home to Anchorage, ignoring Dad's sidelong glances. A few days later a letter arrived from Phyllis. *Dearlings, We now have $8.75. Don't laugh, that's pretty good for 1 week. Besides a fund, there's something else you should be doing, and that is making lists of all the things or places you want to see and do. Every time you come down or I go up I'll copy the lists in the little black "Drive in '65" book I have started. Then every once in a while we'll consolidate the lists and try to map out a route to take so we can see the mostest for the leastest.*

I was ten years old when we hatched this plan, and I had been Outside—meaning out of Alaska—only once. My younger sister and brother had never been to the Lower 48 states nor even much beyond Anchorage and the Kenai Peninsula.

My Aunt Phyllis's kids, Jim and Michelle (known as Mikie then, or sometimes just Mike), were more experienced. Though they lived in tiny Moose Pass, their family had driven down the Alcan Highway and back to visit Uncle Bill's family in Colorado, a journey of 3,400 miles.

Aunt Phyllis and Mom imagined piling their kids into a van, adapted for camping. From the initial goal of visiting Aunt Betty and the New York cousins, the plan grew to cover the length and width of the continent and include places we had only read about in *National Geographic* or *Time* magazine.

My aunts and uncles raised their eyebrows and stared, some with admiration and others with disbelief. A few friends encouraged them to go for it, but sidelong glances betrayed their skepticism.

Uncle Bill snickered through a lopsided grin. My dad scoffed, rolled his eyes. "You'd turn around before you reached the Canadian border," Dad taunted.

Which is to say, they threw fuel on the fire, and the dream of The Drive in '65 blazed to life.

Deep inside, that other voice, the voice of doubt, whispered sweet nothings in their ears, but Mom and Aunt Phyllis refused to listen.

My mom, Winnie Reed, was twenty-nine years old, married with three children, and gainfully employed. Yet no bank would issue her a credit card in her own name. In most states, she couldn't serve on a jury nor be prescribed birth control pills. The doors of Princeton, Harvard, Dartmouth, and Columbia were barred to her, and all women, except in the rarest of circumstances. Her employers paid her less than they paid men who did similar work. Still, Mom dreamed of seeing more of the world. So she saved any spare money and added to our list of travel dreams: jazz music in New Orleans, oranges picked right from the trees.

For several months, with every weekend visit to Moose Pass, Mom and Phyllis gathered all of us together for brainstorming. Where did we most want to go? Each of us had wonders in mind: Surfing! The Empire State Building! The cliff dwellings! By early 1964, Phyllis had purchased a van and negotiated with her husband, Bill, to modify it for our needs. We needed places for everyone to sleep and rooftop storage.

What could we, the kids, do to earn spending money for the trip?

I sometimes babysat to earn money, and since we had the Friday before Easter off school, Marlie and I walked a half mile to a babysitting job with our friend Becky, watching five little kids in an apartment on Minnesota Drive while their mother ran errands. We tried to keep the toddlers amused, and played games with the older kids.

Then a table lamp tipped over.

I looked up. Which child knocked that down?

A floor lamp rocked back and forth, with nobody near it. Becky, Marlie, and I exchanged glances with a shocked awareness.

Earthquake!

"Sandy, quick! Under the table!" Becky said, as she shoved the baby into my arms. We urged the kids to safety while the floor shifted and rolled beneath our feet. A sewing machine on the table teetered dangerously.

"Save it!" cried the oldest boy. "Mom needs it for her sewing jobs."

Marlie hefted the fifteen-pound sewing machine. Straining with all her ten-year-old might, she lowered it to the floor. She yanked the chairs away and rushed to join me and the kids beneath the table.

The concrete floor became a carnival ride. The four-plex groaned. Dishes shattered into broken heaps. The kids screamed in terror, shaken by the earth.

Quakes were familiar to us, but unlike the usual temblors that lasted only seconds, this one rumbled more than four minutes. We waited it out, comforting the children as best we could with our own voices shaking.

Finally, the earth stilled. Silence.

We crept out. Lamps lay on the concrete floor, now streaked with cracks. Shards of dishes and food from counters and cabinets littered the kitchen. The children's few toys were flung around the rooms. The power had failed, and the little remaining afternoon light reflected off the snow outside. As we gazed in shocked silence, the baby wailed, echoed by the shrill wail of sirens outside.

Earthquakes are a fact of life in Alaska, especially along the southern coast. I didn't think too much about its severity or the damage beyond the apartment where we waited. With no injuries to tend, we cleaned up broken dishes and food, tried to distract the children, and waited anxiously for their mom to return.

As darkness fell nearly an hour later, the children's mother burst through the door.

"Where are the kids?" she demanded, panicky until she saw them all. She hugged each one just to be sure. "What did you do when the quake started?"

We described our ordeal, with excited comments from the kids, but she stopped us, clearly angry. "You stayed in the house? Why didn't you take them outside?"

I couldn't understand that—we had done what we had been taught in earthquake drills at school, and her children were all safe, unharmed. However, none of us wanted an argument. We quickly split the babysitting money with Becky, all of us eager to return home.

Marlie and I donned boots and coats and walked through twilight brightened by snow. Lights should have shone in the stores, with the bright windows of nearby houses lighting our way. Instead, all was eerily dark and silent, broken by an occasional car or distant siren. We pointed out to each other the damage around us—broken windows in our neighborhood grocery store and tilting power poles. Someone walked around one house shining a flashlight on the foundation. And was that a whiff of natural gas in the air?

Our house escaped major damage—the concrete porch tilted away from the front door a couple of inches, and the basement floor had a few cracks. But like everyone else, we had no power, phone, or natural gas.

With their children accounted for, Mom and Dad began trying to contact family members on the Kenai Peninsula. All communication was cut off—highways, the railroad, phones, all disabled. They drove to the Red Cross office and signed up for news of our relatives in Moose Pass, Kenai, and Homer. Then we waited but with plenty to do.

In our chilly kitchen, we fixed sandwiches and thermoses of coffee, which Mom and Dad delivered to the workmen repairing roads and docks in Anchorage. A couple of days after the quake, they let me ride along with them. I gaped at the destruction and began to understand the anxiety and anger of the woman we'd been babysitting for. She had been downtown that day, where streets cracked open, buildings collapsed, and broken glass and rubble surrounded her. She picked her way home through a maze of blocked roads, probably imagining the worst for her family.

Three friends whose home suffered major damage stayed at our house, where we used the hamburger starting to thaw in our freezer to cook big pots of goulash and chili on a Coleman camp stove in the garage. Fortunately, we had a water source in the yard—the snow lay several inches deep, so we melted and boiled it for drinking, cooking, and washing. School closed for ten days; for a few schools, even longer.

Dad worked for a trucking company, and its work halted because of all the damaged roads. The major shipping port at Seward, where road, rail, and sea cargo changed hands, was destroyed by a tsunami generated by the earthquake. Successive thirty- and forty-foot waves spread flaming oil from the port's storage tanks across the city.

Mom also worked in transportation, in the offices of SeaLand Services near the Port of Anchorage. Port reconstruction roared along around the clock for months, and she returned to work in makeshift offices a couple of weeks after the earthquake, with restored communications and utilities.

Most of the bridges along the Seward Highway collapsed by the quake. The Army initiated Operation Helping Hand, flying hundreds of missions delivering supplies and machinery as well as taking aerial photos of the damage to the inaccessible railroads and highways to document needed repairs. As shipping routes were rearranged and temporary bridges set up, Dad worked long hours with his company over the ensuing months to keep freight moving.

During the first few days, relief flooded through us each time a family member from Moose Pass, Homer, Kenai, or Seward contacted us. All were safe, but the quake disrupted their lives. Uncle Bill in Moose Pass worked for the Alaska Railroad, which no longer had service through Moose Pass due to earthquake damage. Shortly after the quake, the railroad transferred him to Whittier where the Mason family lived part of the summer of 1964. Whittier's deep-water port had suffered far less damage than Seward. By fall, Uncle Bill was transferred to Anchorage—and for the first time in several years, we lived near enough to walk to their house.

Though we imagined traveling the country end to end the following summer, a more immediate challenge lay closer at hand: the road out of Moose Pass was nearly impassable. Crews started repairing bridges and, within a few weeks, limited travel resumed. Workers replaced bridges along Turnagain Arm with temporary, low crossings, which could be used only at low tide. Traffic stacked up in long lines behind pilot cars, waiting for limited highway openings. As the tides rose, travelers raced to reach the crossings and avoid being stranded until the tide receded.

Turnagain Arm has the highest tides in the U.S.A. (a fact drilled into us in elementary school geography lessons) and a tidal bore that can—on any day—bring in a fast-moving wave several feet high. Until better bridges could be rebuilt, the low-tide crossings and ongoing road repairs lengthened the trip from Anchorage to Moose Pass, normally two hours, to an ordeal twice that long, timed at the mercy of the tidal schedule.

My parents worked well together when faced with a common goal like their business or the earthquake recovery, and their marriage seemed pretty happy most of the time. But in their moments of friction I wondered how happy they really were. By this age, I could count to nine, and I knew they'd been married only six months when I was born. Mom turned eighteen a month before my birth, and finished high school by correspondence. When they argued, I began to question whether they'd have been happier if I never came along. Those arguments passed, and my questions faded, until the next time.

And what about our plans for the Drive? When we finally visited Aunt Phyllis a couple of weeks after the earthquake, she described their terrifying experience, watching the water in Trail Lake slosh up to the highway twenty feet above the normal level of the lake. Trees swayed wildly, bending nearly to the ground. "Our van bounced all over my driveway. I could see it from the house," she said. Fortunately, it stayed upright and escaped damage, unlike so many cars we had seen crushed by collapsed buildings or tilted into yawning cracks in the roads.

Only a couple of months earlier, Phyllis had bought a brand-new Chevy Greenbrier van—a model that would later be rated among the worst cars produced that year, part of the Corvair series of vehicles reamed by consumer watchdog Ralph Nader as "Unsafe at any Speed." It had a rear-end air-cooled engine, and the front bench seat perched above the front wheels. The tan and white van was as plain as sand, but we had ideas for spiffing it up.

Despite his ongoing mockery of our plans, Uncle Bill agreed to customize the van with a roll-up tent canopy over the side double doors, and the slide-out extension out the back doors, where my cousin Jim and I would sleep. The three younger kids, Marlie and Glenn, and my cousin Mikie, would sleep on the bench seats. Mom, Phyllis, and Gram would sleep on folding aluminum lawn loungers under the side canopy—a striped canvas roof with walls of mosquito netting.

In May, Phyllis sent a letter addressed to "Miss Sandra Reed, Sec'y Drive in 65" to let me know that Mikie was summarizing our finances for a treasurer's report. Phyllis also reported that travel information from around the country filled her mailbox, and we could soon compile it to formulate our plans for the route we would follow. In addition, Phyllis illustrated with a few sketches her ideas for the car-top storage bin and roll-up tent.

With our classes back in session, life slowly adapted to a new normal. Would that new normal allow for the trip we had planned? This was a topic of many discussions among Mom, Dad, Phyllis, and Bill over beer and pinochle as the fall of 1964 approached.

To bolster their case, Mom and Phyllis developed a financial plan. They presented the cost of meals and household expenses for two families at Alaska prices if we stayed home. The alternative: our dads would pay for our gas bills—only thirty cents a gallon—charged to a credit card, but our savings would pay the rest of our expenses while we traveled. Surely Dad and Uncle Bill could see how much money they would save if we traveled for fourteen weeks rather than burden them with the expense of feeding and maintaining us all at home.

Mom and Phyllis applied their usual creativity and determination to the plan, and they prevailed. The Drive was on!

Meanwhile in news of the wider world, Sydney Poitier won an Academy Award for Best Actor in *Lilies of the Field*—"the first of his race" as the *Anchorage Daily Times* reported, to be so honored. And race proved big news that year, with the Civil Rights Act of 1964 taking effect in July. The import of that act escaped me, a white twelve-year-old living far from the scene of demonstrations and conflict.

Alaska, vast as it was, had left me small in important ways—small in my perception of other people in the world, those whose color and culture were strange to me. My school had a handful of black students and very few of Latino or Native American descent. Just as strange to me were the inhabitants of crowded cities, and anyone who spent life in the sweltering heat and humidity of the South—people who had never seen snow.

I frowned at the grainy television images of protests, riots, and President Lyndon Johnson signing the new law. How would this important new law affect those angry, bleeding protesters? How would it affect me? I was too far removed to know, but The Drive in '65 was about to shake up my world.

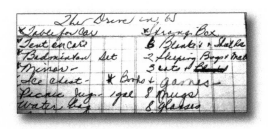

Chapter 2

Marilyn Reed   *Jan. 1, 1965*
New Years Resolution List
This year I will try to make my grades higher so I can go on the drive. I will try to behave on the drive. I want to play like my cousin Mikie Mason and I are twins. We want to be good sports on the drive in '65. I won't spend very much money (if I can help it).

MY SISTER, MARLIE, and our cousin Mikie, two months apart in age, had been playmates all their lives. They celebrated their eleventh birthdays a few months before our planned departure in May, and I was twelve when Marlie wrote her New Year's resolutions. My grades were already very good, and my behavior exemplary—so much so that Marlie once told visitors, "Sandy's so good she won't even say 'beaver dam'."

Thanks to the earthquake, Phyllis's family moved to Anchorage by the time school started in the fall of 1964. Marlie and Mikie became nearly inseparable.

The two girls set up a Barbie doll kingdom in our mostly unfinished basement, chalking elaborate house plans on the concrete floor and rearranging the doll furniture. Barbie sweaters and shoes, accoutrements of all sorts, littered an area the size of a small bedroom.

Their Barbie obsession led Marlie to write a request addressed "Dear Limitits" which referred to Mom and Aunt Phyllis, who placed limits on everything that could be brought on the trip.

"We would like to know if we may each take 3 Barbie type dolls on the drive in '65. We will also take a few things and buy a few things on the way (if okayed). Thank You. Truley Yours, Marilyn Reed"

We each prepared a small suitcase, smaller than today's typical carry-on luggage, closer to the size of a large briefcase. In it all our clothes, personal items, diary, and toys had to fit. The adults also worked out their limits. Aunt Phyllis, always inclined to flamboyant appearance, wrangled with Mom about bringing her jewelry. The jewelry made the cut.

Marlie, Glenn, and I were all born in Seward before Alaska became a state, as were Jim and Mikie. My dad applied for a government homesite—through a variation of the homestead acts begun in 1862—that contained five acres on the south end of Moose Pass, along the highway between Seward and Anchorage. Dad built a small house with hand-pumped water and an oil heater in the living room. We lived in Moose Pass for my first five years. Our house had electricity but no telephone. Moose wandered through our yard to a nearby salt lick.

My mother's father, Grandpa Sanders, died in that house in May 1957. He and Gram were babysitting several grandchildren while Mom and Dad attended a ball game in Seward with a group of family members. When Grandpa had a heart attack, no one could call for help. Gram sent me, the oldest child there at five years old, up to the highway to flag down a car and ride to the store for help. Moose Pass had no doctor, clinic, or ambulance—nothing closer than Seward, thirty miles away. At the store, the clerk called the community emergency crew, local residents trained in first aid. By the time they arrived, Grandpa had died.

Dad's parents, Merle and Opal Reed, lived a mile or so away in 'downtown' Moose Pass, near the railroad station and Estes Brothers store and gas station, owned by Mom's sister Nancy and her husband. A short boardwalk connected my grandparents' home and business, a jewelry manufacturing shop. In that dusty, dimly lit room filled with mysterious equipment, Grandpa cast tiny gold charms and soldered gold nuggets onto cast gold shapes. He forbade children to enter the shop, but when I was ten, Grandpa guided me to one of the work stations and instructed me in the finer points of soldering gold nuggets on my own initial 'S', dipping each nugget in greenish liquid flux before placing it on the gold base and passing the blowtorch's flame over it a few times.

Grandma Opal, Dad's mother, died of breast cancer in 1956, and Grandpa Reed soon married her sister Lela. They were the only married people I knew who slept in twin beds. Lela's daughter Jackie became step-sister to my Uncle Paul, dad's brother. According to family lore, Grandpa Reed proposed to Lela by saying they should marry since they both had teenagers to raise. Not the most romantic approach, but they remained happily married until he died about twenty years later.

Mom's sister Phyllis, always my favorite aunt, was thirty-eight years old in 1965, the eldest   of seven siblings. My cousin Jim was born of her first marriage to a man who had been a prisoner of the Japanese during World War II and drank too much. The marriage didn't last. She married Uncle Bill in 1953 and soon had her daughter, Mikie. In Moose Pass, Phyllis worked   for   my   dad's father   at   his   jewelry manufacturing shop, keeping his books and traveling for occasional sales trips. At home she followed crafting   trends,   and   sometimes invented   her   own.   Knit,   crochet, macramé,   basket-weaving—she   loved   trying something new and experimented to add her own flair to each project. She and a friend crafted earrings from moose turds coated with shellac, and the local store sold them to tourists.

Phyllis Mason

Most of our family holiday gatherings filled her house in Moose Pass, where she had a baby grand piano and a gardenia plant whose exotic perfume wafted through her large living room when it bloomed. Anything that amused Phyllis brought a burst of laughter, and her curiosity about life and the world proved contagious. In her book collection I could always find something interesting. Often as not I climbed upstairs to a low-ceilinged bedroom and sat in a hug-me chair by the gable window, transported by classic children's stories or big Time-Life coffee table books.

After Grandpa Sanders died in 1957, Gram (her name was actually Mary Sanders) moved in with Phyllis and Bill, and she baked homemade bread

Sandy Reed

for them every week. If we visited on bread-making day, Gram would heat lard in a cast iron skillet and fry bits of bread dough for the kids, a treat I considered superior to most. Gram worked for another jewelry manufacturer in town, a neighbor of Phyllis's, and soldered gold nuggets onto cast gold initials in a tiny shop.

A favorite conversation with Gram, for almost any of her grandchildren, would begin with one request: "Gram, tell us about the olden days!"

Mary "Gram" Sanders

She shared tales of her early life in Patchogue, New York, where her Italian father worked in a lace factory, and stories of raising her young family in Smithtown. About sewing piecework for an underwear factory while Grandpa worked out of town. About seeing a child trampled by a horse, which gave her a lifelong fear of horses.

24

I loved listening, and Gram let me brush her hair and fix it in crazy braids, ponytails, and hair clips while she talked about her brothers and sisters, school days, and the house her father built using no nails.

In 1965, twenty years after bringing her seven children to Alaska, and about a week before our departure on the Drive, Gram turned fifty-eight. She was the matriarch of a thriving family but far more a follower than a leader, always agreeable, and sometimes passive to a maddening degree. She disliked conflict so would agree with both parties in any argument, which drove Mom crazy.

Phyllis truly filled the role of matriarch, gathering the clan at her home, pulling together group activities, from agate hunting forays to family reunions that grew over the years to more than a hundred people. Gram joined every gathering, the honored elder, but Phyllis ran the show.

My mom, Winnie Reed (later known as Win), was Phyllis's faithful sidekick. The sixth of seven kids, Mom was seven years younger than Phyllis, the firstborn. She told me many times that Phyllis was always her hero. When their family left New York to move to Alaska in 1945, Mom was eleven and Phyllis eighteen, olive-skinned and black-haired, the dark Italian beauty Mom always envied.

They grew up in a home devoid of books. Mom never read a book just for the pleasure of it until after she married. Gram and

Winnie Reed

25

Grandpa both grew up in New York, in immigrant families, neither educated beyond eighth grade. Gram plucked "newspapers" from the sensational tabloid racks.

In Seward, Alaska, when Mom was thirteen, doctors diagnosed the wife of her dad's best friend with tuberculosis and quarantined her at the local sanatorium. Grandpa sent Mom to live at their house and care for their young children—while continuing her own schooling. Her family lived nearby, but she lived away from home, earning her own money, and coping with the responsibility of running a household for the next four years.

Gram and Grandpa doted on their youngest daughter, Betty, indulging her in every way. If Betty accepted a babysitting job and then didn't want to do it when the time arrived, Grandpa sent Mom in her place, whether she wanted the job or had other plans. Mom, only seventeen months older than Betty, grew up feeling expendable in a family where the love was spread thin.

In 1965, Aunt Phyllis's son, Jim, was fifteen, two years older than I, with a year-round tan and straight white teeth. Aware of his own good looks, he started to develop a swagger. A three-month trip with all the younger kids sounded like a bore to him, and he knew he would be the official tire changer and heavy lifter the entire way. Hormones and teen attitude created some conflict with his mother, and sometimes with the rest of us, but I was glad to have

Jim Clark

him along. In Alaska, he joined in play and mischief with a couple of boy cousins his age and older, and dismissed the rest of us as little kids. But among our band of travelers, he and I were the older kids, and our bond as cousins grew stronger.

Two years earlier, a motorcycle accident broke his pelvis, trapping him in traction for many weeks. A year before the Drive, as his family prepared to move from Moose Pass to Anchorage after the earthquake, Jim accidentally shot and killed his closest friend. That traumatic event dogged him all his life.

Marlie and Mikie were twins for the Drive, and they loved nothing better than finding ways to embarrass me. A favorite trick: when we parked or drove in slow traffic, they would whistle or call out to a boy nearby, and then duck behind me so it appeared I had catcalled. Marlie could be counted on to do the unexpected. As we walked home from elementary school, she once dragged along a

Marlie Reed

section of picket fence she found in the ditch. Another day, she claimed an empty liquor bottle, the kind with the handle formed into the glass.

Mikie Mason

Mikie's contagious giggle brightened every gathering, and she could lighten the tone in tense moments by finding the humor in any situation. Her happy outlook and quick smile made her a fun but at times precocious companion, and she brought all that along on the Drive.

My brother, Glenn, wore his trademark smile most of the time and grinned at the prospect of all the discoveries awaiting us that summer. At nine years old he was ready—like all of us—to experience new places and new things such as body surfing, meeting the legendary family members from Mom's and Gram's stories, and Disneyland. He wasn't expecting the searing sunburns, cactus milkshakes, nor stepping on a wasp nest.

Glenn Reed

Our preparations continued through the winter and into the next season, known as breakup in Alaska. Not quite spring, breakup melted the old snow into slush and mud, revealing the trash that storms and society threw about during the winter months. As the frozen ground, hard as bedrock, thawed to muck we gathered our gear, packed and repacked our satchels, and purchased spare tires, fan belts, and tarps for the van. Along the roadsides, snow berms plowed up during the winter months gradually shrunk and grayed with the grime of auto exhaust, dust, and debris. Spring might mean daffodils and tulips somewhere else, but breakup in Alaska was a dirty business.

Mom stoked our excitement with every mention of the coming Drive. "We'll meet all kinds of people. A stranger is just a friend you haven't met yet." Meanwhile, Dad sat back with his beer, muttering an occasional warning that not everyone was as friendly as they seemed. Mom poo-pooed his concern, assuring us of great times ahead, meeting people all over the country. Mom requested permission from the schools to let us leave before the year ended, and our teachers agreed we would learn more on the trip than during those last two weeks in classrooms.

The evening of May 21 was worse than Christmas Eve at our house. Anticipation kept us restless during the night, and we rose before six, sleepy-eyed and a little cranky. With our camping gear packed in the van already, we checked our satchels, gripping them as we stared out the sliding glass door watching for Phyllis and the van. She and her family arrived before seven o'clock, wearing the same groggy expressions.

Dad and Uncle Bill joked about expecting us home before dinnertime, but we determined to show them. Soon we gave final hugs. The photo taken May 22, 1965, the day we drove away, showed the van in the back yard of our house in Anchorage, loaded up, including a roof rack. We all hung out the windows waving goodbye, Phyllis behind the wheel in sunglasses, Glenn in the back seat punching a fist in the air. Then we drove out, heading up Spenard Road, driving our first mile of thousands. My insides roiled with anticipation as we passed through Anchorage toward the Matanuska Valley, then beyond all familiar territory and into the unknown.

Ahead of us, summer awaited, a summer of adventure. Like Lewis and Clark's Corps of Discovery, we were off to explore the strange land that was our own country.

EVENTS AND PLACES VISITED

Date *Saturday - May 22, 1965*

Place *Anchorage*

Weather *overcast   45°*

Blast off time ! 7:00 A

Mileage on car: 13,295.9

Chapter 3

HALFHEARTED FROM OUR SLEEPLESS NIGHT, we sang a few songs, but the mood of the group was not particularly festive. Phyllis, Mom, and Jim, riding in the front seat, began waving to the cars we met. Over the next few days, we decided to conduct a social experiment. We would determine the friendliest of the twenty-five states and six Canadian provinces we drove through based on how many people waved back to us in each place. Waving, and noting the responses, became the job of whoever rode in front.

Most of the two-lane road within Alaska to the Canadian border was paved by 1965. Paved does not mean smooth. Frost heaves, created when water seeps into the gravel road bed and then freezes and thaws, caused the road to rise or drop like a roller-coaster. We jounced over them that early spring day, because summer repair work hadn't yet started. Most shoulders offered only a foot or so of extra space.

Although a road connecting Alaska to the Lower 48 had been discussed since at least 1930, the Japanese attack on Pearl Harbor in December 1941 jolted the military into action. The War Department recognized Alaska's vulnerability and began surveying in February 1942.

Because of the vegetation, terrain, and eighteen inches of snow, the survey crew covered only two to four miles per day. Within six months, the Japanese had attacked Alaska's Aleutian archipelago and soon occupied the American islands of Attu and Kiska. Road building began at a frenzied pace, with the goal of building a pioneer road for supply trucks as quickly as humanly possible.

In June 1942, the same month as the invasion of the Aleutians, the U.S. Army assigned seven engineering regiments, each to construct a three hundred-fifty-mile stretch of road. With no roads and few airfields along the route, dog teams and horses hauled in supplies. The long daylight hours allowed crews to work twenty-four hours a day in eight-hour shifts. They constructed timber trestle bridges across two hundred rivers, and some of those bridges lasted until the 1980s.

The work teams completed more than fifteen hundred miles of road in six months, between June and November 1942.

By 1965 Alaska's population had grown to about 270,000—almost triple the population two decades earlier. Although improved a lot from that initial supply road, the Alcan remained a two thousand-mile narrow track through the wilderness. Oil and gas development was in its infancy. Exploration had not yet revealed the vast oil reserves of the far north that would place Prudhoe Bay and the Alaska pipeline on the map.

Even today, with three times the 1965 population, the vastness of the state is hard to appreciate. When we drove away that spring, the roads built across it were little more than widened trails. In stretches of hundreds of miles, only an occasional roadhouse or lone gas pump in front of a small store broke up the surrounding wilderness. Buildings might be constructed of logs, or whatever kind of lumber could be milled there or trucked to the site. Travel required planning for many contingencies and filling the gas tank at every opportunity. Running out of gas meant waiting for a Good Samaritan, on a route with very few Samaritans at all.

Alaska is known for logging, with its images of enormous spruce, fir, and cedar. Along the route of the Glenn, Richardson, and Alcan highways, black spruce is the more common tree. This is one of the least attractive evergreens in all creation, a scrawny pillar of a tree with little to recommend it. I suspect Dr. Seuss used them as a model when he illustrated the Christmas trees in his Grinch book. My father cut one of these and brought it home for Christmas in 1961, resulting in tears and outrage from my mother. It was truly pathetic, as family photos testify.

We enjoyed a landscape of black spruce through much of the two thousand miles from Anchorage to Edmonton, Alberta. Muskeg populated with black spruce and cottonwood, covering hundreds of thousands of square miles.

After blasting off from Anchorage at 7 a.m. on May 22, we arrived at Canadian customs at 7 p.m., having put more than five hundred miles behind us on the first day. We stopped for the night about fifty miles into Canada's Yukon Territory at Lake Creek campground.

We set up our van just as planned, working fast as the evening chill settled around us. Mom fixed us a quick supper of sandwiches and hot cocoa. After unloading the back end, Jim and I set up our sleeping area. The van's double rear doors opened to a cargo area, which sat directly above the rear-mounted engine covered by a flat metal access door. That's where we stored our suitcases and camping gear as we traveled. The cargo area wasn't big enough for anyone to sleep in, but Uncle Bill had rigged up a plywood extension that pulled out. Notches on each side held it in place, level, forming a sleeping platform for me and Jim, with our heads over the engine compartment and our feet out the back door.

We rolled out our sleeping bags. The younger kids bedded down on the three bench seats. With the side double doors open, a tent of canvas and mosquito netting rolled out to enclose the lawn loungers where the adults puttered around, arranging their sleeping bags and settling in for the night. Peace descended, briefly.

Hysterical laughter from Mom and Phyllis soon propelled us all upright again.

Aunt Phyllis described the scene in a letter home: *"All I can see of Mama is two feet sticking straight up and a profusion of bedroll and pillows where her head should be—two arms flailing wildly—I can see now in this dim light and through tears in my eyes that her cot has folded up around her. But she hasn't uttered a sound. (You know, she never cusses.) Winnie has mustered the strength to compose herself from mounting hysteria and is untangling Mama. We had spent at least 15 minutes tonight explaining to Mama how these lounge chairs work. When you mount them the weight must be centered. Once you have accomplished this you can stretch out with ease and confidence. Apparently Mama put too much weight aforedeck and her aft ascended.*"

Finally we all slept, unconcerned about the news of the day and cut off from the rest of our family. That night, beyond the border of Alaska, I lay in my sleeping bag trying to picture what we might see tomorrow. My mind wandered down the map. What was the rest of Canada like? How soon would we reach warmer temperatures? And what adventures waited down the road?

We woke early in freezing weather. Mom and Phyllis grumbled about it, and I pulled my jeans into the sleeping bag to warm them up. As I dressed, Phyllis's words gladdened my heart.

"It's too bloody cold to cook out here," Phyllis groused. "Let's find a restaurant for breakfast."

Jim and I pushed our plywood bed over the engine hatch so the rear storage area could be filled, while Mom and Phyllis organized the cooler, rolled up their sleeping bags, and stowed the three aluminum loungers on the roof. We left our warm coats at home to save space, so we doubled up with sweaters under our summer jackets and shivered as we packed. With everything crammed in, we huddled together in the back seat while Mom drove for an hour or so to a lodge along the road where we could eat breakfast.

We knew we'd gone through a time zone change, but when we looked at the clock in the dining room, it read 12:20 p.m. We had never heard of "double daylight savings time," but the Yukon Territory used it. Instead of a one-hour adjustment for daylight savings, they adjusted two hours. Combined with the time zone change from Alaska, we had to change our clocks and watches three hours. Our motto, painted across the van's back doors, read "The hurrier we go the behinder we get," and it suited the day perfectly. We ate breakfast for lunch and carried on.

Soon after crossing the Canadian border the previous night, we left pavement behind and spent the next three days rattling through the Yukon Territory and British Columbia's hinterlands on gravel roads.

Mom and Phyllis prepared for this. They distributed surgical face masks to all of us, so dust couldn't seep into our lungs and sinuses. More than a thousand miles stretched ahead of us before we would reach pavement again.

Driving through a whole lot more of nothing, Phyllis said, "Who wants to stop at a ghost town?"

With our clamor of yesses, she pulled onto a side road at the south end of Kluane Lake. The day had warmed from its frosty beginning. We eagerly explored Silver City, a cluster of dilapidated cabins and wagons. We scampered from one to another, peering skeptically at the sagging roofs before testing the rotting floorboards. Jim and Glenn climbed onto the seat of an old wagon and pantomimed driving a team of horses, hauling freight and mail in gold rush days. Originally a miners' way station around 1900 to 1920, Silver City served as a camp during Alcan Highway construction.

Most of those primitive buildings and log cabins collapsed years ago, but they stood sturdily enough then for us to walk through and wonder who had lived there, and if perhaps anyone had left a gold poke buried beneath the floor boards.

Silver City lacked an outhouse, but we Alaskans knew how to use a screen of bushes for privacy.

That night we arrived at Whitehorse, having covered another three hundred miles, and stayed at a private campground where, for two dollars, we had a camping space with firewood, running water, and hot showers—our first since we left home. Laundry cost only twenty-five cents a load, so we washed everything that needed it.

Alaska's status as the largest state in the union, more than twice the size of Texas, was a matter of pride to all of us Alaskan-born kids. When we set up camp, our customized van with Alaska license plates and crew of women and children always drew attention. We bragged on Alaska at every opportunity—which is especially easy to do when you have no other experience to draw on. Someone remarked to my cousin Jim about the size of an extra-large cookie he was eating.

With a casual glance and slight shrug, Jim bragged, "Everything's big in Alaska."

He didn't mention we bought the cookies just up the road, before pulling into camp for the night.

We were prepared for primitive camping, but Mom and Phyllis brought along the essentials of civilized living. Mom offered the man camped next to us a martini, prepared in her cocktail shaker and served in stemware, as she and Phyllis answered his questions about living and working in Alaska.

Both Phyllis and Mom began a near-daily ritual of writing a letter home each evening, telling of the day's events. Already they envisioned writing a book together about the adventures ahead of us. Dad and Bill promised to save all our letters, a means of documenting our travels. Among those early letters,

Phyllis began referring to our van as the Wayward Bus, and the name stuck.

The next morning our laundry hung frozen stiff on the clothesline, and adding to the inconvenience, we discovered our van had two flat tires. Two! Dad and Uncle Bill thought a challenge like this would change our minds about the trip, but no. We had two spares on top of the car and hauled them down. Jim muttered curses but bent to the task of changing the flats in the icy morning air. The rest of us shivered and helped as we could, waiting to pack the van, and doubting the assurances of Mom and Phyllis that we would soon be complaining of the heat. Finally, we eased back onto the gravel road and headed south. Behind a face mask that caused my glasses to fog up, I dreamed of the warm summer weather ahead.

Along the way, we spotted wildlife—moose, caribou, even a bear—a dead one, loaded on top of a passing car. We also saw bighorn sheep close to the highway. Their brown color surprised me: the only wild sheep I had seen before were the white Dall sheep that populated the Kenai Peninsula.

Every so often we passed a road sign saying "Watch for grader approaching in your lane." Why would the grader be approaching in our lane? Couldn't the road be graded in the same direction as the traffic? Phyl and Mom were baffled. They discussed the mystery and never found a satisfactory explanation—but the signs continued to appear. However, the grader never did approach in our lane.

That day, May 24, we covered four hundred miles and stopped for the night at Liard Hot Springs in northern British Columbia. We donned our swimsuits for the first time, and in spite of the chilly air and a mild smell of rotten eggs, the hot sulfur spring water relaxed us all. We wanted to make it a bubble bath, but Mom and Phyllis put the kibosh on that, knowing the tiniest sliver of soap might bury us in foam.

As kids in Alaska, our swimming opportunities were extremely limited. Moose Pass had a small pond near the railroad station, not much more than a glorified mud puddle but its small size helped it to warm up a bit under the weak summer sun. About five miles north of town, an abandoned gravel pit fed by melting snow provided a bigger swimming hole, if you didn't mind swimming in ice water. I did mind. And the rocky lake bottom threatened to cut our feet. Ocean beaches were far too cold and dangerous.

For real luxury in water experiences, we might go to Goose Lake in Anchorage. Developed in the late 1950s for public recreation, the shallow water actually warmed up a little in the summer, with lifeguards and real sand along the shore. But that was miles away across town from our house, and with two working parents, we didn't go often.

Anchorage had one indoor swimming pool in the early 1960s called The Spa. Seventh-grade physical education curriculum in Anchorage schools included six weeks of swimming instruction there. School buses hauled us to our obligatory lessons, lumbering into the Chester Creek valley south of downtown. The big glass building with steamy windows intimidated me, and I hated sliding into the pool. I advanced to the dog-paddle, shivering even in the heated water, and then shuffled out into the freezing cold for the return bus ride to school. Dodge ball or calisthenics in the gym, in the blue rompers they called our gym uniform, suited me better than swimming ever would.

None of us kids could swim well, though Jim swam better than the rest. He was certainly stronger and more athletic. Liard Hot Springs didn't call for actual swimming, though. All of us immersed ourselves in the water for a relaxing soak that transformed us into glowing noodles, ready for dreamland. Something even I could enjoy.

We spent that night in a couple of cabins, a welcome change after the frozen clothes and flat tires of the last couple of days. Warm and rested the next morning, we carried on waving to the cars we met on the road south.

Phyllis wrote, in a letter to Uncle Bill: *"We had gone thru Fort Nelson and were merrily rolling along waving to everyone as usual, then stopped for dinner at Prophet River Lodge. As we were leaving, the waitress asked if either of us was Mrs. Reed or Mrs. Mason, as there was a long distance phone call for us. For a few terrifying moments we thought something terrible had happened back in Anchorage. (Who else could locate us?) Well, it was none other than our old friend Clyde Jackson [a family friend]... on his way back from a trip to Mexico. He had seen us waving and thought we'd recognized him too. He had turned around and tried in vain to catch us, then had turned back toward home and phoned from Fort Nelson."*

That day Mom and Phyllis decided to push all the way to Dawson Creek, British Columbia, ten hours or more from Liard Hot Springs, so we drove long into the night.

I never liked sleeping in the car. As we approached Dawson Creek, I hung my arms over the front bench seat and looked out the front window into the darkness. All around me on the two back bench seats, the other kids and grandma dozed. Mom gripped the steering wheel and glanced back at me. "Do you notice anything different?" she asked.

I looked around, unsure what she meant.

"What do you hear?" she hinted.

Nothing. Then I realized how quiet it was. "Pavement!"

Finally, the gravel roads lay behind us. We drove into Dawson Creek, population about 12,000, making it the biggest town since we left Anchorage. We had come to the end—or more properly, the beginning—of the Alcan. Milepost 0, where construction began more than twenty years earlier.

It was midnight, and the road felt soft as a cloud.

Chapter 4

WITH ALL THE MILES OF ROUGH ROAD we'd traveled, Mom and Phyllis decided we would stay two nights in Dawson Creek and have the car serviced, do some shopping, and find a laundromat. So the morning after our late arrival, we dropped off the car at the service station and ate a late breakfast at a Chinese restaurant. The eight of us were the only patrons at 10 a.m. and the waiters gathered around with rapt attention as we shared our plans for the summer. Our orders of bacon and eggs, pancakes, toast, and coffee absorbed the aromas of chow mein and won ton soup, giving the ordinary breakfast an exotic flavor. By the time we finished, even the cook and manager had joined the conversation, and all lined up to wish us well as we left. The bill for our eight breakfasts totaled less than five dollars.

In Dawson Creek we purchased another car top carrier, to help create a little more room inside the van. After trying to install it on their own for a couple of hours, Mom and Phyllis returned to the service station for help, a most fortunate decision. In the course of their earlier servicing of our van, the mechanics had removed the plywood bed extension— where Jim and I slept—and neglected to put it back in. Now they installed the car top carrier and returned our piece of plywood.

At one of these early stops in Canada, we purchased another embellishment to our Wayward Bus. Stick-on animal tracks now ran up one side, over the roof, and down the other side.

Much of the shopping had to be put off because at that time Dawson Creek had an ordinance making Wednesday afternoon a holiday, so most of the stores were closed. What kind of crazy law was that?

We prepared the van for an early departure the next morning and visited with more people at the campground on their way to Alaska, always full of questions. Now, however, our attention focused on our first U.S. destination: Ashland, Wisconsin. My father's grandmother lived there, along with some aunts, uncles, and cousins. After so many miles cooped up in the car, we wanted the time and space to visit people, even virtual strangers, and enjoy activity.

The weather warmed noticeably, with green grass and trees leafing out—the kind of weather Alaska wouldn't see until mid-June or later, and here in Canada spring arrived earlier, by May 27. Living in Alaska all of my twelve summers, I'd seen snow as late as my birthday in the first week of May. Yes, grass turned green and trees grew leaves in the summer, but the ground always felt cold to bare feet. And the streams or lakes we swam in, like the old gravel pit near Moose Pass, filled with melting snow and glaciers each summer. I'd heard that sizzling heat could make a sidewalk so hot you could fry an egg on it, but that had to be a myth. Based on my life experience, nothing seemed so unlikely.

As we traveled southeast, we marveled at the warming soil beneath our feet and the thriving agriculture that soil supported. Our letters home mentioned the cows and horses we passed as if we viewed the national treasures of Canada. But we had never seen hundreds of domestic animals at a time, like the herds of cattle on the Canadian prairies that week.

The wild animals we knew of traveled mostly alone—individual moose, bear, porcupines. Groups of sheep and goats on the mountainsides rarely numbered more than a dozen or two. Large caribou herds live in Alaska, but we had never seen them. The Kenai Peninsula caribou were long gone by 1960 due to overhunting and habitat loss from wildfires. Four herds are back in the area today after being reintroduced in the 1960s and 1980s.

Mom and Phyllis approached Edmonton with anxious discussions of the best route through the city. How would they deal with traffic in a metropolis of nearly 400,000? They had never driven in a city larger than Anchorage, with fewer than 50,000 people.

Mom took the wheel. Phyllis handled the map and watched for highway signs. In the back, we gaped.

"Look at that building!"

"I never saw so many cars."

"What's the road we're looking for?"

Phyllis hissed for quiet, but that didn't stop us. Marlie and Glenn stared out at the largest city they'd ever seen.

The noise level inside the van rose as we pointed out the shopping centers, many lanes of traffic with overpasses and complicated intersections, and cars whizzing all around us.

Phyllis wrote home to Uncle Bill, saying, *"I wasn't aware of the degree of panicky atmosphere I had created until Jim slapped down Glennie's hand as he was excitedly pointing at a beautiful tall apt. building. Jim screeched, 'Don't point, you'll distract the driver!' This had the effect of a cold washcloth on our fevered brows and we sheepishly relaxed a little and made our way through the city without getting lost or killed or even hardly noticed."*

In a journal we kept our plans and expenses for the trip, and one heading reads "Rules of Agreement for Conduct in traveling." Rule number one: "Do not bother the driver! Do not touch the driver. Do not yell or throw things." Travel through Edmonton gave us our first real test of that rule.

At a campground east of Edmonton, after a seventy-degree afternoon, lush green pastures surrounded us. We fell asleep to the unfamiliar sounds of crickets, punctuated by an occasional low moo.

The next day we began the longest stretch of driving on our trip so far. We crossed all of Saskatchewan and Manitoba, nearly nine hundred miles, with Mom and Phyllis taking turns driving. When night fell, the rest of us slept as best we could, leaning on the shoulder or lap next to us as we traveled through the Canadian farmlands.

Mom's diary notes: *"Drove all night. Won't do that again."*

As we drove across the prairies of Canada, the United States headed into Memorial Day weekend, with warnings in many newspapers to drive carefully. Seat belts would not be mandatory equipment in automobiles until 1968. Newspaper headlines the next Tuesday reported the highest holiday weekend traffic death toll ever recorded: 474 people had died in accidents between 6 p.m. Friday and midnight Monday in the United States.

Annual car sales in the U.S. had nearly doubled from 1951, when recordkeeping began, to 1965, when 9.3 million cars were sold.

In recent years, the Memorial Day weekend traffic death toll has rarely surpassed 400. Along with mandatory seat belts, use of airbags, and constant improvements to vehicle safety, the nation's roads themselves have been improved. The interstate highway system, constructed between the late 1950s and mid-1970s, allows long distance travel with limited access. Roundabouts, rumble strips, and improved guardrail design all contribute to safer road travel in America.

After the long drive from Edmonton, two days and all night in between, everyone wanted out. Out of the car and space to move. At Kenora, Ontario, on the shore of Lake of the Woods, we rented an A-frame cabin with two bedrooms, a bathroom and kitchen plus living area, at the Harbor View Motel. Our deck overlooked a boardwalk and dock on the waterfront.

Maybe nostalgia plays into my fond memories of Kenora, because our letters home compare the location to Moose Pass and Trail Lake, the lake of our childhood. That comparison just shows how little we knew about Lake of the Woods. It is enormous, with a surface area of nearly 1,700 square miles. Trail Lake covers only a few square miles. More than 14,000 islands dot the surface of Lake of the Woods, and the shoreline including the islands stretches 65,000 miles.

None of that mattered to us. We wanted nothing more than to stretch and move, to enjoy the lake and the warm day. Mom and Phyllis cooked a simple meal, something like tuna and noodles with a fresh salad, in the luxury of a real kitchen instead of a campground. Jim rented a small motorboat with his own money, and Mom filmed movies of him giving rides to us younger kids. We explored the bay in front of our cabin, which beat swimming—one waggling toe in the water proved it too cold even for our Alaskan sensitivities.

From Kenora, Mom phoned my dad's grandmother, Anna Reed, in Ashland, Wisconsin, to let her know we would be arriving the next day.

"What do you kids want to do when we are in Wisconsin?" Mom asked when she finished the call.

Jim grumbled something about wanting to stay out of the van for a couple of days.

"I want to go to the cheese factory!" Marlie shouted then looked to Mikie, who gave a little shrug of tentative agreement.

"That sounds interesting," I said, wondering what kind of alchemy changed milk into cheese.

The van needed a thorough cleaning after eight days of steady use, and we unpacked, reorganized, and repacked like a jigsaw puzzle, so it all fit snugly. We had camped enough by then to appreciate the luxury of sleeping in beds, or even on sofas or floors, with all the legroom we needed. Hot running water added to the sense of luxury as we cleaned up in the morning.

Finally, we pulled up to the border crossing at International Falls, Minnesota. The customs agent eyed us through the windows then glanced up at our roof rack storage and the footprint stickers up the side of the van. He called to a colleague and spoke a few words we couldn't hear, even with the driver's side window rolled down.

"Good morning, ma'am," he said, strolling to the window. "Where are you headed?"

I can just imagine the answer Phyllis gave. "We're just taking the kids on a camping trip." Or maybe, "We're going to visit relatives in New York. Did we make a wrong turn?"

"Are you all U. S. citizens?"

No one needed a passport for travel to Canada or Mexico at that time, and none of us had yet been issued one. Phyllis confirmed our American citizenship as requested, but border protocol required a few more questions.

"How long were you in Canada?"

"Just as long as it takes to drive from the Alaska border. About a week."

They soon sent us on our way with best wishes for a summer of fun. After lunch at a drive-in, we continued another four hours or so, with mounting excitement at meeting more of our distant family and spending a couple of days out of the car.

Our travel rules stipulated what expenses our pooled money would cover. These included "food & grog, lodging, film, stamps & writing materials including postcards, various entertainments." Thanks to vigilant record-keeping, I know that we spent fifteen dollars on the lakefront cabin in Kenora, and rarely as much as five dollars to fill the tank with gas.

We grabbed a newspaper at Kenora. I enjoyed catching up on the space race. Astronaut Ed White's proposed spacewalk included an attempt to approach an orbiting spent rocket—the first rendezvous in space. Headlines also announced the U.S. bombing of Hon Nieu Island off Vietnam, destroying an anti-aircraft battery and radar tower. And the *Ottawa Journal* reported that Adlai Stevenson, America's ambassador to the United Nations, faced students protesting U.S. policies in Vietnam as he entered the University of Toronto for a dinner and presentation.

Chapter 5

ASHLAND, ON THE SHORE OF LAKE SUPERIOR, was home to Dad's grandmother, his Uncle Wayne, and Aunt Donna. Wayne and Donna's children were near my age, even though they were my dad's first cousins. My Grandpa Reed's sister Beulah and her husband lived on a farm in the country, the same place their parents had farmed until Great-Grandpa Reed died in 1954.

I had traveled to Ashland in 1961, at age nine, with Gram. I enjoyed this benefit of my privileged position as the eldest child in my family, and the eldest grandchild of my father's parents, and the eldest great-grandchild by far of Great-Grandma Anna in Ashland. I imagine (though of course I don't recall clearly) that I was a prig about this.

My parents had bought me a mouton fur parka to wear on that trip in 1961. Mouton is sheep fleece treated to resemble wild animal furs, a less expensive alternative to traditional fur parkas. The beautiful coat kept me warm in Wisconsin. One of the uncles picked us up in Minneapolis and drove us to Ashland, where we stayed at Great-Grandma Anna's house.

Her bathroom had a claw-foot tub, where Gram and I bathed together. When we finished in the tub, Gram said, "Have you heard of that new dance, the twist?" I had, but at nine I wasn't tuned in to the latest dances yet. She described it for me. "They say you move your arms like you're drying your back with a bath towel and rub your foot on the floor like you're putting out a cigarette on the ground." And we practiced the twist with our towels before we dressed for bed. In 1961, our visit to Wisconsin lasted only a couple of days, then Gram and I flew on to Washington, D.C., where I sweltered in that mouton parka through the Christmas holiday with Aunt Betty, Mom and Phyllis's youngest sister, and her family.

During my winter visit in 1961, Wisconsin had cold weather and snow on the ground—a lot like Alaska. In June it barely seemed like the same place, with everything green and warm.

Our Wayward Bus arrived at Wayne and Donna's house on the night of their son Craig's high school graduation, May 30. All the local relatives gathered to celebrate the occasion, so we met everyone in one fell swoop. They welcomed us to join the celebratory dinner, a good time for us to begin sorting out who was who. I spent that night with cousin Gail, and Jim stayed over at Uncle Wayne's house with cousin Bruce. The Wayward Bus carried all the rest to Great-Grandma Anna's house.

The next day we visited Great-Aunt Beulah's farm in Highbridge, where we learned about ticks.

Alaska had summer mosquitos, but harbored no ticks, chiggers, or similar nuisances. We listened to vivid descriptions of how a tick could dig its head into you and swell up as it sucked your blood. About how you might put a hot match to the back end of a tick to force it to release its grip—and hope that the head didn't break off when you pulled on it, so it stayed under your skin and could lead to life-threatening blood poisoning. Whether anyone actually said this, or we just imagined it as we listened, I don't know.

We played on the farm, enjoying the open spaces, a pasture with a few cows, and trees to climb. After taking her turn climbing a big pine tree, Mikie dropped from a low branch to the ground and ran screaming toward the house. I understood just one word: "Tick!"

In the kitchen, she flung herself around, thrashing her arms so nobody could catch hold of her. The rest of us trailed after her, crowding in at the kitchen door.

Mom tried to grab her.

Phyllis hollered, "Hold still and tell us what's wrong!"

Finally Mom gripped an arm and pulled her into a big hug. "Now tell us what's the matter."

Through sobs, she choked out, "There's a tick on me!"

Gram looked her over. "It's just a little tick," she said, parting the hair on Mikie's scalp to expose it. Gram had experience with such things from when they lived in New York, before the move to Alaska in 1945. She plucked the tick off Mikie's head. "Look, it's just this little thing."

Mikie wiped her eyes, shrinking back from the tick Gram held out to her. "Kill it!"

The tick was dispatched, but nobody wanted to go back outside, knowing now that the horror stories were true. We settled down in front of the black-and-white television to watch *Bonanza*.

Mom's diary discloses that Dad had visited his relatives in Wisconsin in 1948, the year he graduated from Fairbanks High School, when both his grandparents lived on the same farm where we had the tick encounter. Having grown up in the mountains of Idaho, and then central Alaska, Dad likely experienced the same newness in Wisconsin that we did visiting the lush green dairy farming region.

Both Great-Grandma Anna and her husband, Harry Reed, grew up in Iowa farm families, and they fell in love despite what their families considered an unbridgeable divide: her family was Roman Catholic and German, and his of Scotch-Irish Protestant descent. The families fought their engagement for many months but eventually relented, and Anna and Harry married in May 1906. He was twenty-three and she only seventeen. Witnesses in the marriage record book were Anna's widowed mother and her brother, Anna's uncle. Had Harry Reed's family boycotted the event? I sometimes wonder if the religious divisions in his family contributed to my Grandpa Reed's lifelong atheism.

In 1965, Anna Reed was our only living great-grandparent, so we stopped in Wisconsin for me, Marlie, and Glenn, more than for the rest of the crew. We three were her only blood relatives in the Wayward Bus. Anna had visited Alaska a couple of years earlier, and the *Anchorage Daily Times* published a four-generation photo of us.

But most of the relatives we met in Wisconsin had never been to Alaska. They exuded a sense of awe as we answered many questions about our lives. People marveled at things that seemed perfectly ordinary to us: the bright summer nights and dark winter days, the bear and moose that sometimes wandered through our yards, Dad's annual hunting trips for mountain goat and Dall sheep to fill our freezer.

Our Wisconsin kin wondered how we could talk so casually about seeing a bear in our yard yet become so hysterical over a tick.

We crammed a lot into two days in Ashland, touring general points of interest such as Copper Falls State Park, and points of family interest—the school Wayne had attended, a big red brick building that seemed as strange to us as an igloo was to them. Alaska construction used little to no brick. In Wisconsin on the first of June, we enjoyed seventy-degree weather—like midsummer to us. We admired the lush gardens. Peas climbed the fences. Beets, broccoli, onions, spinach, and lettuce stood ready to harvest, while Alaska's gardens were just being planted.

A letter from Dad arrived for us in Wisconsin. It included a thousand-dollar check for Mom as a result of a house deal he had finalized—maybe the sale of the house we had moved from a year and a half earlier. He shared very brief news of his work and an expansion of Grandpa Reed's jewelry manufacturing shop in Moose Pass. He hadn't received any of our earlier letters or postcards when he wrote to us on May 28. The letter included nothing particularly warm and personal for Mom, but he asked where he should send his next letter, and closed with *Love, Lyle.*

What visit to Wisconsin would be complete without seeing a cheese factory? On our last night in Canada, Marlie wrote to Dad saying she wanted to visit one with Wayne and Donna. A couple of days later, she wrote him again: *"Uncle Wayne took us to a cheese factory. I couldn't stay in there very long because it stank!"*

Marlie was right, of course. Mom described it as "the warm sweet smell of sour." I stuck it out, despite the ripe aroma, watching two men with long paddles turn over the curds as they formed in a giant stainless steel vat filled with milk. We ate some of the fresh curds, unimpressed with their flavorless rubbery texture. We left the cheese to age and continued our Wisconsin adventures.

Marlie, Mikie, and Glenn spent one day exploring Ashland with Great-Grandma Anna. According to Marlie's letter, Anna took them all to town and "We had a blast!" They didn't want to say what they had done—Marlie and Mikie loved keeping secrets. I imagined treats at an ice cream store, playing at a park, maybe taking a closer look at enormous Lake Superior.

Wayne and Donna drove the rest of us to Duluth, Minnesota, seventy miles away, for a shopping spree at Minnesota Woolen Company. Duluth boasted twice the population of Anchorage, and the discount stores held racks and tables filled with clothes much cheaper than Alaska prices.

The shopping trip was quite a blast for Mom. She noted in her diary, *"Spent $100 on clothes (would have cost $250.00 not on sale)."*

My own letter to Dad contained more details: *"We got lots of school clothes that we are sending to you. I got lots of nice skirts & sweaters. Mom got a new mandolin from Uncle Wayne. We are having lots of fun. Make lots of money to pay our bills. (HA! HA!) Love ya, Sandy"*

Mom had always purchased our school clothes from mail order catalogs. J.C. Penney opened a department store in Anchorage in 1962, but we had shopped there only a few times before the 1964 earthquake destroyed it. I spent many childhood hours perusing the Montgomery Ward and Sears & Roebuck catalogs, dreaming of a wardrobe that, in reality, devolved to a few practical items and maybe one special selection each fall. J.C. Penney first offered catalog sales in 1963—late to the game compared to Sears and Wards.

My Grandma and Grandpa Reed lived in Moose Pass and had matching leather recliners in their living room. On a table between the chairs, Grandpa Reed kept a humidor filled with his aromatic pipe tobacco. An attached rack held a few pipes. And on a bookshelf to the left of his chair, the most recent Sears catalog, two inches thick and offering birdhouses, boats, and beautiful clothes, sat in easy reach of even me. There I daydreamed, during many visits to my grandparents' house, breathing in the scents of leather and pipe tobacco, imagining the clothes I'd wear to school, to parties, or out to play. Those aromas are forever linked in my mind with the fun of catalog shopping.

The opportunity to see the clothes in person, and at such discounted prices, exceeded all my catalog dreams. No wonder we piled our cart high and mailed home boxes of clothes.

On June 2 we drove from Ashland to Milwaukee, where Dad's Uncle Glen lived in the suburb of Wauwatosa. As we passed through Phillips, Wisconsin, Phyllis braked and pointed. "What on God's green earth is that?"

We all stretched toward the windows, stunned to see life-sized concrete figures of men and women, a team of oxen, and a pair of hunting dogs, embedded with bits of colored glass from bottles for flair.

"Stop! Let's go look!" we clamored, and Phyllis obliged. Her own creative spirit sprang to life as we wandered among the cowboys and Indians, a wedding party in a horse-drawn surrey, and Paul Bunyan-style lumberjacks.

This was all the creation of Fred Smith, born in 1886 to German immigrants who settled near Phillips. Fred worked in logging, sold ginseng, raised Christmas trees, and started a tavern. When he retired in the 1940s, he began creating his concrete figures. In 1964, as he completed a set of full-scale Clydesdale horses pulling a beer wagon, Fred suffered a stroke. Though he recovered, Fred didn't add anything more to his roadside attraction. He passed away in 1976.

Fred Smith's Wisconsin Concrete Park still draws people off the road to examine one man's whimsy. It's rated the top attraction in Phillips, Wisconsin, on TripAdvisor and elicited great reviews on Google too.

We carried on to Wauwatosa, arriving after dark, and encountered a freeway cloverleaf that nearly trapped us in a never-ending circuit of on-ramps and off-ramps. After three or four loop-de-loops, accompanied by high-decibel guidance from every member of our party, we found our way off in the right direction and arrived a little worse for wear at Uncle Glen and Aunt Cookie's house about 10 p.m.

While most of us slept on sofas, floors, or guest beds, Mom stayed up visiting with Glen and Cookie until 2:30 a.m. Their favorite hobby was dancing, something Mom enjoyed, too. Dad's uncle Glen was only six years older than Dad.

Uncle Glen owned a delicatessen near Milwaukee. We visited it briefly the morning of June 3, and they stocked us with cold cuts, sliced cheese, and deli bread for lunch, before we headed to the shore of Lake Michigan and the next leg of our journey.

Chapter 6

ON A POSTCARD TO DAD, Glenn scrawled: *I am on the boat in this picture. I am going across Lake Michigan. It is 2:00 and it goes 8 miles an hour. It is a hundred miles across.*

The postcard pictures the SS *Badger*, a coal-powered steamship that launched on Lake Michigan in 1952, built as a rail, auto, and passenger ferry. Part of the Chesapeake and Ohio rail system, the *Badger* carried us from Milwaukee to Ludington, Michigan. I gaped in astonishment as railcars rolled on board. Soon we joined the line of vehicles and drove right onto the ship ourselves.

To erase any doubt about what a nerdy kid I was, I present this letter written to my dad.

Dear Daddy,

I thought you would like to know about this ferry we are on. It is very big. I talked with a man who works on this boat and I learned about it. The gross tonnage is about 4,000 and the net about 2,000 tons, the displacement tonnage is 8,500 tons. It has 7,000 horsepower with twin screws. One propeller weighs 15,000 pounds and it cost 4 million dollars to build the whole boat. It is over 400 feet long and lots of people and trains and cars can fit. They use them for ice breakers too, just like in Cook Inlet. I don't suppose any of this stuff will help me in 8th grade. It's nice to ride the ferry for a change from driving but I'm getting sick so I'll close.

Love, Sandy

The *Badger*, named for the University of Wisconsin mascot, changed hands in the 1980s, and in 1990 it was the last remaining rail and auto ferry when it was laid up, ending rail ferry service on the lake. A year or so later it was purchased and refitted to serve only auto and passenger traffic.

Early in 2016 the SS *Badger* achieved the status of a National Historic Landmark. It now crosses Lake Michigan on a different route, between Ludington and Manitowoc, Wisconsin. Tripadviser.com has more than 700 reviews, most of them five stars, and lists the *Badger* as the fourth most popular thing to do in Ludington.

After our cruise across the lake we searched out a campground as we headed east into rural northern Michigan. We found a small state park with camping spots, very peaceful and in fact all but empty on that weeknight, and early in the season. We chose a spot not far from the only other camper in the whole place, because we could swim in a nearby pond.

The other camper, a man alone, offered us his fire and said he was leaving. We gladly moved into his site, and while we kids swam in the pond, Mom, Phyllis, and Gram drove to a nearby store for supplies.

The man watched us swimming, and then asked if he could leave a couple of things at the campsite.

We agreed and thought nothing of it, though when our moms returned, they thought it a little odd. Why didn't he just keep his belongings with him so he wouldn't need to come back later? When they walked to the pond to watch us splashing around, the sight of his tent set up again on the other side of the water surprised them. He strolled over and talked with them about Alaska and Michigan then returned around the pond as we started our dinner.

Soon the stars appeared, and time for bed. After our swim, most of us fell asleep quickly. Mom and Phyllis stretched out on their aluminum cots next to Gram. As the quiet of the night seeped in around them, Mom whispered, "Wasn't that guy a little strange?"

Gram nodded. "I wish there were more campers here."

Phyllis paused a minute, then whispered, "Should we leave?"

"Let's not be ridiculous," Mom offered in a quavering voice. "There are eight of us, after all, and we haven't even slept yet."

By this time all three stared wide-eyed into the night through the mosquito netting, listening to every blowing leaf and squirrel's footstep. In the course of a few minutes the soft-spoken man had become a predator preparing his attack on us from his hideout across the pond.

The three of them agreed to take turns staying awake, standing watch so the others could sleep. As they conferred, Phyllis said, "Wait! What was that noise?"

"What noise?"

"Shut up and listen!"

"I can't hear anything."

"What did it sound like?"

"I don't know. Winnie, get the flashlight."

As Mom gripped the flashlight and took a step, she tripped over a transistor radio, falling against the open side of the van and jostling the sleeping kids. Whatever caused the noise, whether rabbit, raccoon, or rising wind, was now long gone.

Now the noise arose inside the van. "Will you guys be quiet?" Jim griped, punching his pillow and flopping onto his other side.

Marlie lifted her head and looked around. "What's the matter now?"

Glenn poked his head over the front seat, frowning at the disturbance.

"Sorry. Everything's fine," Mom lied. "Go back to sleep."

We drifted off again, ignorant of the looming danger.

Phyllis took the first watch and described it this way: *The axe murderer had no doubt relaxed on his haunches waiting patiently for us to quiet down again. With every nerve alive and my life's supply of adrenalin surging to meet the foe, I was to just lie there 'til I got sleepy, then wake up Mom or Win. Five minutes passed. Five minutes filled with the strange night sounds of a strange unfriendly place. I heard the footfalls of a panther and the heartbeat of a timber wolf close by. Every few moments I caught a glimpse of the night sky through the trees as they bent in brewing storm, but try as I might, my eyes could not pierce the black velvet night smothering us and I had to rely solely on my ears so that very soon I had to quit breathing almost entirely as I was making so much noise and might miss something important. Into this quiet watchfulness came the explosion of something dreadful in Winnie's area. "WHAAAT?" I screamed, sitting bolt upright.*

"Shut up, you idiot," Winnie hissed. "I just slapped a mosquito."

None of them slept. As dawn lightened the sky, they felt a bit foolish, and even more exhausted. They woke us all at about 6 a.m. and we packed up our camp as quietly as we could, then stole away.

Like zombies, Mom and Phyllis took turns driving across Michigan and through Ontario, Canada, to Niagara Falls, where we rented nice secure hotel rooms. We kids wondered what made them so crabby that day, and eventually they shared the whole story. For more than fifty years, we have recounted our narrow escape from the axe murderer in the north woods of Michigan.

While we headed for Michigan June 3, Ed White of the Gemini 4 mission walked in space over the Pacific Ocean, the first American spacewalker. The *Ludington (Michigan) Daily News* proclaimed in bold headlines, "Space Walk is Big Success." Similar articles dominated front pages across America. Each night the rising moon reminded us of the space race, and our nation's goal to land a man on the moon before the Russians did. And each space mission was a tangible step toward that ultimate "giant leap for mankind" yet to come.

Down the page, below the fold, the paper reported the murder of a black deputy, shot, along with his partner, in their patrol car in Bogalusa, Louisiana. "The Negros were hired recently by Sheriff Dorman A. Crowe to patrol the Negro sections—a move that brought angry condemnation from the Ku Klux Klan," the article reported. Nearly a week of racial conflict had yielded fifty arrests after black demonstrators demanded better pay and employment opportunities.

When I pointed out the story to Phyllis, she read it in silence and handed it back, lips pursed. "I hope we don't run into anything like that down south."

Me too, I thought.

Chapter 7

I STARED OPENMOUTHED at the television screen in June 1963, not even knowing what question to ask. In the photo, a man sat cross-legged on the ground as flames rose from his clothing and over his head, spreading on the pavement around him. After being drenched in gasoline, he had lit the match himself. The extremity of his actions baffled me, and I didn't understand the religious conflict that reportedly inspired it. One question repeated in my mind: how could that help?

Between mid-June and mid-August 1963, five Buddhist monks protested the South Vietnamese government's treatment of Buddhists by publicly burning themselves to death. That image of Thich Quang Duc became one of the iconic photos from the 1960s.

In the years before 1965, very little news of Vietnam penetrated my world. Yes, America had some "advisors" there, and the news carried occasional stories of casualties. Between 1956 and 1964, nearly five hundred American military personnel died in Vietnam. But I had homework to do, friends to meet, and odd jobs to earn money for our trip.

In January 1965, Secretary of Defense Robert McNamara and National Security Advisor McGeorge Bundy met with President Johnson to discuss what is known as "the fork in the road memo" about changing U.S. policy regarding Vietnam. We knew nothing of that at the time, but the decisions resulting from that memo would affect everyone in our Wayward Bus.

March of 1965 brought a heightened protest of the war, when Alice Herz, an eighty-two-year-old peace activist, set herself on fire on a Detroit street corner and died a few days later. Several other large protests happened that spring around the country. My twelve-year-old mind could not see any path to making sense of it. Detroit was not a faraway and foreign place like Saigon. Opposing the war? Yes, I heard both sides of that debate at family gatherings and saw both sides on the news. But I could see no blaze of glory in suicide.

Mom and Phyllis discussed the buildup of troops in Vietnam and the increasingly common reports of military deaths. They expressed sadness and anger that the U.S. was involved.

"I'm just glad," Aunt Phyllis said, "that this is happening now, when our kids are too young to go."

For the first time, it occurred to me that someone from my own family might be sent there. Jim was fifteen years old then, Glenn only nine. Phyllis's comment calmed my initial anxiety, but then I thought of my oldest cousin, Frank Estes, two years older than Jim. He had only one more year of high school. I clung to a shaky hope that America's involvement in Vietnam would bring a speedy end to the conflict.

Throughout 1965, the United States drafted more and more young American men into military service and sent them to Asia. At the beginning of that year, U.S. military personnel in South Vietnam numbered about 23,000. By the end of the year, that number ballooned to more than 185,000.

In 1968, the year Jim graduated from high school, America's involvement peaked at 536,100 troops. Jim was not inclined to academics, nor college-bound, and by then every young man eighteen years old waited, often with fear and trembling, for his draft number to come up. Rather than be drafted into the Army, Jim joined the Air Force. By then our cousin Frank was already serving in the Navy. Jim served his basic training in Texas.

In June 1964, three months after the Good Friday earthquake, I was in Moose Pass, helping Aunt Phyllis prepare to move. Jim packed gear for a final camping trip with his best friend, Bruce, before moving to Anchorage.

Growing up in rural Alaska, Jim had used guns since childhood. With a backpack slung over one shoulder, he hugged his sleeping bag with one arm and held his .22 with his free hand.

In the kitchen he laid the rifle on the table and grabbed some food, shoving some in the backpack and some in his mouth. As he hoisted the .22 again, Phyllis nagged. "Did you check that gun? You shouldn't carry it out there loaded."

"I know what I'm doing, Ma. Would you get off my back?"

Within hours, his friend lay dying in the hospital, hit in the head as he and Jim took shots at each other from behind trees near their camping spot, Jim using the rifle he'd been so certain was not loaded.

Someone brought Jim home to Phyllis and Bill's house. He slammed into his bedroom. Dread filled me as adults gathered and spoke in hushed tones, awaiting news from the hospital in Seward, but without much hope. I kept quiet, fearing yet wanting to know what had happened. Afraid I would be sent upstairs or to the neighbors' house if I asked. I watched from a corner of the living room, mute, as Jim carried his BB gun and another rifle to the fireplace, weeping, and tried to stuff them in, even though they were too long to fit, wanting to burn them and be finished with guns.

Every gun safety talk in the community hall, hundreds of admonitions never to point a gun at another person, weighed on Jim like boulders. He knew he and Bruce had broken all the rules, and his best friend had paid with his life. I wonder how many times Jim replayed those instructions, and his mother's nagging question, in his mind over the next forty years.

In his Air Force training, he took up a gun again. He excelled at marksmanship, winning awards among his fellow trainees. But sometimes, late at night, he would call home, emotions unraveling, telling his mother he didn't want the awards. That every time he looked at the target he saw Bruce's face.

PTSD wasn't added to the American Psychiatric Association's Diagnostic and Statistical Manual of Mental Disorders until 1980, but it has been documented by various names throughout history. Jim carried the effects of a traumatic accident with him to the Air Force, to Vietnam, self-medicating with drugs and alcohol, and back into civilian life, marriages and divorces. In middle age, his life smoothed out, and he became a loving and fun-loving father and family man. While the trauma healed, scars remained, perhaps visible only to those closest to him.

The escalating war in Vietnam played in the background throughout our travels, when we happened to see a newspaper or catch the TV news. And the protests escalated in equal measure. Mom opposed the war in conversation and admired those who were brave enough to demonstrate their opposition to America's involvement.

If asked at that time to describe Ho Chi Minh, I'd have called him a puppet of the Chinese government, trying to expand its communist influence into Southeast Asia. That was the American government script. But I knew so little.

I didn't know that Ho Chi Minh, with a small group of Vietnamese nationalists, had contacted President Woodrow Wilson in 1919 at the Versailles Peace Conference, seeking support for Vietnamese independence from the colonial rule of France. America ignored them.

I didn't know that he turned to examine the Soviet and Chinese governments only after this rebuff. During years of exile from his homeland, he traveled to Europe, America, the Soviet Union, and China. Finally in 1941 he returned to Vietnam, and secretly pulled together a group of nationalists to free his country from colonial rule.

I didn't know that during World War II the Office of Strategic Services (forerunner of the CIA) sought out Ho Chi Minh as a source of intelligence on the Japanese in Southeast Asia during the final months of the war. He provided very good, useful intelligence, according to Lt. Col. Archimedes Patti, and asked in exchange an open line of communication with the Allies.

I didn't know that when proclaiming the independence of Vietnam to half a million people gathered in Hanoi in September 1945, he quoted from America's Declaration of Independence.

As we crossed North America, loosely tracking the news, I didn't know that the previous forty-five years were marked with missed opportunities for interactions with Vietnam that might have avoided American military involvement and the loss of so many lives, entirely.

With the focus on stopping the spread of communism, most of the American public supported our involvement. Would that have changed if more people had known? Government documents continue to be declassified, providing a very different picture of the situation in Vietnam than the news reports of 1965.

As we dipped back into the United States at Niagara Falls on the night of June 4, we saw a rainbow of colored lights on the water. The next morning we visited the falls, of which I took several poor-quality photos: blurry, fingertip intruding into the viewfinder, people too far away to identify, or camera tilted. The roar of water provided background music as we searched the length of the fence for the best view and looked through the telescopes.

I watched the *Maid of the Mist* plying the water below the falls and wished we had the time and money for all of us to go aboard for a cruise, despite the promise of a wet ride in the heavy mist. She was a nearly new vessel, the previous two "Maids" having been destroyed by fire started by a welder's spark in 1955. I had to settle for the magnificent view from above.

In the early afternoon, we continued eastward and found a motel in Geneva, New York, at the northern end of Seneca Lake. We arrived early enough for the necessities that were becoming routine: taking the car to be serviced and finding a laundromat for our clothes. When Mom picked up the car, the young service station attendant could not contain his many questions about Alaska, finally asking sheepishly, "Do the Eskimos really live in igloos?"

People surprised us with their ignorance of Alaska, and the misinformation accepted as fact by so many. No doubt some people today still picture Eskimos living in snow domes along the Arctic coast. We gladly answered questions. Their impressions of life in Alaska stemmed from nature movies or Jack London stories. Our understanding focused on frozen water pipes and cars too cold to start, and sometimes our answers disappointed them.

We couldn't help but laugh at what people in New York or Texas called mountains, after a lifetime within sight of the rocky crags of Chugach National Forest. Those little hills? They were far from mountains in our book.

I'm sure our ignorance of their areas shocked them. I envisioned the coastline of southern California as an uninterrupted stretch of palm-lined beaches, with no allowance for the commercial dockyards, rocky cliffs, or estuaries that actually mark the coast.

We kids helped fold the laundry, hurrying Mom and Gram. Back at the motel, a swimming pool awaited. After an eighty-degree day, the hottest my siblings and I had ever experienced, we could hardly wait. In a flash, we kids donned our swimsuits and raced out the door to enjoy the first motel pool of the trip. For me, Marlie, and Glenn, it was a first in our lives. As the afternoon cooled, we splashed in clear clean water and rested on the grassy verge, enjoying the goodness of life.

Mikie wrote to Uncle Bill: *"We swam at night and in the morning. I slid off the slide about a dozen times. Marlie and Glenn were afraid to."* With our transistor radio by the pool, we listened to "Wooly Bully" by Sam the Sham and the Pharoahs, "Help Me, Rhonda" by the Beach Boys, and the Rolling Stones' brand new song, "Satisfaction."

Out in the world that day, the Yankees beat the White Sox 12-0 at Yankee Stadium in front of 33,000 people. The only professional sport we'd ever seen was the World Championship Sled Dog Race held each February in Anchorage during the annual Fur Rendezvous. I would have been hard-pressed to name any pro baseball player of the day, but I loved to cheer for George Attla, the Huslia Hustler. He'd won the mushing championship in 1958 and 1962, and would go on to win it eight more times. The thousand-mile Iditarod Race, launched in 1973, took the spotlight in dog mushing. George Attla raced to a fourth-place finish in the inaugural Iditarod.

Even today, Alaska hosts a few semipro but no professional sports teams. Dog mushing is the official state sport.

In news from farther south, 2,500 spectators gathered in Trenton, North Carolina, as Knights of the

Chapter 7

Ku Klux Klan marched around a fifty-foot burning cross at the closing ceremonies of a rally. The Klan experienced a dramatic drop in membership from a peak in 1925, after its inner workings were exposed and some courts convicted prominent leaders of felonies. As racial tensions rose in the early 1960s, Klan membership grew somewhat, and cross-burning rallies in the rural south became more frequent. Newspapers published photos of these events, and I hoped we could avoid those people when we traveled through the Deep South.

Chapter 8

E VEN AT THIRTEEN, I loved history. Alaska's history barely counted, it all happened so recently. Now we headed to the East Coast and some real history. The *Mayflower* landed right here. Colonists fought for America's freedom right here. I could hardly wait.

On June 7 we drove into Boston, eager to see Harvard University. Phyllis had imagined a spacious campus but Harvard's buildings crowded together like the rest of the crowded city. I felt claustrophobic with *"the buildings all hooked together"* as I wrote to Dad, with no grass or flowers.

We certainly viewed Harvard from every angle. Each time we tried to move on, the streets just kept taking us past another part of it, or sometimes past a part we had already seen.

In the back of the car we kids fretted, a little angry that the adults in charge didn't know the way. And we were cranky in the ninety-degree heat. Mom and Phyllis found our anger and anxiety funny. "We have three months to find our way home," they blithely assured us. Sometimes, like that day in Boston, we feared it might take that long.

We finally escaped the clutches of Harvard. In the heat of the day, we dozed in the car and woke up when it stopped. Outside we could see the dockyards at Boston Harbor, and a network of bays and peninsulas beyond. Mom and Phyllis rustled the map between them and debated the best route out of town, laughing as their wrong turns became obvious.

There, among the trucks, ships, and trains on their maze of railroad tracks, two cops pulled up. What now? Mom and Phyllis stopped laughing.

When the officers approached our car, though, their smiles reassured us. Their first question: "Did you gals come all the way from *Alasker* in this rig?"

I struggled to understand the brogue as Mom and Phyllis answered their questions. We relaxed when it became clear that the cops' interest was motivated by curiosity and a desire to help. We were obviously lost, and the officers gave us a police escort to the highway out of town. Mom's diary does not even mention our brief visit to Boston.

Our next stop that day—and the biggest disappointment of the trip, bar none—was Plymouth Rock. I had an image in my mind of a great rock on the shore of Massachusetts, a landmark guiding the Pilgrims to safe harbor, and which, afterward, they had engraved with the year of their landing as a memorial stone.

I recently read that the original rock spanned about fifteen feet long and three feet wide and weighed about twenty thousand pounds. The rock we drove all those miles to see was not half that big. Probably not one-fourth.

My brother, Glenn, summed up our collective reaction. "Is that Plymouth Rock?" he said. "That little thing would fit in our bathtub!"

Housed in a portico like a small temple, possibly to add some sense of grandeur to the unimpressive stone, Plymouth Rock sits along the shore of Cape Cod Bay. Pieces of the rock are now found in several places: the Smithsonian in Washington, D.C., Pilgrim Hall Museum in Plymouth, and the Plymouth Church of the Pilgrims in Brooklyn Heights, New York, all own pieces. Souvenir scraps of the rock are probably cached in attics and featured on mantels around the country, too, from previous periods when it was less protected.

The pitiful remainder lies on the shore in Plymouth. The date carved upon it is not the work of Pilgrims—it was not carved into the rock until 1880. In fact, nothing is mentioned about the rock in written records of the Pilgrims, until the mid-1700s, more than a hundred years after their arrival. The Pilgrim landing grew into a legend, and the fame of the rock rose with it.

The Pilgrims actually first landed at Cape Cod, near what is now Provincetown, Massachusetts, in November 1620, and a few weeks later traveled across the wide bay to where Plymouth now stands. Two hundred yards from the rock, they established their settlement.

We also toured replica of the *Mayflower*, built to scale, which had been completed in England and in 1957 sailed from Plymouth, Devon, to Plymouth, Massachusetts. I tried to imagine the 1620 voyage, which brought one hundred two travelers in that tiny ship, only one hundred six feet long and twenty-five feet wide.

My boating experience prior to the Lake Michigan ferry was limited to salmon fishing outings in Uncle Bill's twenty-five-foot cabin cruiser in Resurrection Bay, outside of Seward. Uncle Bill's aluminum boat banged over the waves at high speed. One year, during the annual Seward Silver Salmon Derby, we camped with Phyllis's family and Gram on one of the many coves of Resurrection Bay. With a good driftwood fire started, we became bored waiting for the boat to return from a fishing jaunt.

"Can we go for a walk, Gram?"

"Help me turn these sleeping bags over. They aren't quite dry yet," Gram said. "I hope it doesn't rain again tonight." We spread them on the large driftwood logs that formed our seats around the campfire. Then we hiked up the beach, looking for shells, agates, and other curiosities.

We returned to find that the wind had shifted, blowing a couple of sleeping bags into the fire, and nearly ending our camping trip.

The Pilgrims also had to deal with shifting winds in their little sailing vessel, as the wind provided their only power. While we disdained the small size of Plymouth Rock, we truly marveled at the small size of the *Mayflower*, and its journey crammed with so many people. A few had come before, but the legend of America (if not the history) counts our nation's beginnings from those few dozen who arrived on the *Mayflower*, the leading vessel for many millions more who followed and called America their home.

We also explored the replica Pilgrim village and discovered several houses were actually gift shops in disguise. The one-way foot traffic through the village prevented us from escaping, like cattle being forced through the chutes I had seen in Rawhide and

Bonanza on television. We looked forward to scrambling back into the van where our aching feet could find relief, and perhaps an Atlantic breeze might even cool our sweltering bodies as we headed for Cape Cod with the windows rolled down.

After driving to the cape, we stopped for dinner at the Orleans Inn, a waterfront eatery and quite a splurge. Dinner for all of us cost $28.07. A sign near the door read "Come as you are," which Mom and Phyllis found inviting for our bedraggled crew, all wearing shorts.

Phyllis wrote: *I'm afraid we did not do justice to Cape Cod and all its romantic history, however we are spending the night in a place called Buzzards Bay! (honest to God). Let me never hear a New Englander make fun of Moose Pass, Alaska.*

Tomorrow we will be in Smithtown [NY]. We plan to stay a week and while we are there Winnie and Mama and I will settle all the arguments we've been having for the past 20 years about the size of Miller's Pond, where did Allison Skipworth live, how many miles to Long Beach, blah, blah, blah. Just can't wait 'til tomorrow!

Family disputes made the news that week too. Book reviews for *The Last Grand Duchess: Her Imperial Highness Grand Duchess Olga Alexandrovna* by Ian Vorres tempted readers with the story of the last Romanov rulers of Russia. Olga, the last tsar's sister, died in exile in 1960. She denied the claims of Anna Anderson, one of several women who said she was the tsar's daughter, Grand Duchess Anastasia, and had survived the regicide. Vorres' book joined many others on the topic, and new books are still being published a hundred years after the murder of Tsar Nicholas and his family. However, the potential survival of Anastasia was conclusively disproved in 2007 when the last remains of the tsar's family were discovered. Historical mysteries like this one intrigued me even then, and I still find them fascinating.

Chapter 9

MOM AND PHYLLIS, and even calm and quiet Gram, grew more excited by the mile as we crossed Rhode Island on June 8, headed to Bridgeport, Connecticut. From there we would catch the ferry to Port Jefferson, New York, on Long Island. Then to Smithtown—the hometown they left behind in 1945—only twelve miles away.

My stomach rose and fell with the waves as we crossed Long Island Sound, but the nausea dissipated quickly after we landed, with the heightened anticipation of meeting Mom's many cousins. These New York relatives peopled childhood tales, told by Gram or Mom or any of our aunts and uncles, and they were legends in our minds.

Jerry Valentine, a cousin about my mom's age, tormented her as a child. In one humiliating incident, he held her against a tree in the yard until she wet her pants, and laughed as she ran home crying. I'll admit to a little anxiety about meeting this thug.

Lo and behold, Jerry Valentine greeted us with hugs, invited us in out of the heat, and offered lemonade or a soda (which we had always called pop). Could this be the villain of Mom's childhood stories? We began to question the reports about him.

Another cousin, George Arns, let us stay in his house—a big vintage home more than one hundred years old, according to a letter Mikie wrote to her dad. Very few structures in Alaska were that old in 1965, and we considered the house a historical treasure. We brought our bags inside and sorted out the sleeping arrangements, which allowed private bedrooms for Mom and Phyllis.

As the sun dropped into the west, and the oppressive heat lifted a little, we gathered outside on the lawn with cold drinks, watching light fade in the neighborhood.

"Hey!" Glenn shouted.

All heads swiveled toward him, but he seemed to be staring across the yard in a trance. "There! Did you see that light?"

"I see it!" I said as a tiny light flashed a few inches above the grass. Then another. Magic spread over the lawn, with flashes of light glowing for a second or two and disappearing into the darkening green. "There's another one." I pointed to a flash of light already fading.

"What is it?" Glenn asked what we all wanted to know.

Mom and Phyllis grinned like kids. "Lightning bugs!" Mom ran into the house and rummaged around the kitchen for a jar. "Catch them in here. They'll make a little lamp for the yard."

We stalked the lawn, capturing the miniature flashlights in our cupped hands and adding them to the mayonnaise jar. The magical moment, the discovery of fireflies, stayed with us for years.

We tested the waters of Long Island Sound on a beach that Mom called Little Africa, one of her childhood haunts. The disgusting seaweed smells brought tears of nostalgia to Mom's eyes. I sunbathed in my first two-piece swimsuit, blue with a white belt at the waist and scalloped edge below my bust.

Through the week we visited so many aunts, uncles, and cousins they melded into a blur. Grandma Sanders had six siblings and Grandpa Sanders had eleven. Many of them still lived on Long Island, with children and grandchildren of their own.

Within a day or two we had met Kathy and Ruth, Rainy and Janey, Elsie, Wally, Florence, Dot, Tony, Frankie, Rose, Teddy and Helen, Billy, Della, and many others of Mom and Phyllis's generation. All those cousins had crowds of children our ages too. Each lunch and dinner we visited one relation's house or another for a picnic, barbecue, or spaghetti feed. They welcomed their long-lost cousins from Alaska. Some had swimming pools in their yards, giving us delightful relief from the heat, which ranged from eighty to ninety degrees all week.

Phyllis recorded her schedule on June 16 for Uncle Bill. She visited an old school friend in the morning, attended a wiener roast at Dot's house at 2:30 p.m., enjoyed cocktails at cousin Jimmy's at five and dinner at Aunt Elsie's at six. After a week of that, she said, *"We'll be glad to get on the road again to rest."*

One humid day Aunt Dot accompanied us to the World's Fair in New York City. We visited the Alaska Pavilion. A giant igloo had been constructed for the

Alaska displays—fortunately not constructed of ice and snow, or it wouldn't survive a New York summer. Wouldn't you know, friends of my mom staffed the exhibit. Totem poles, which had originally been carved for the St. Louis World's Fair held in 1904, stood guard over the Indian and Eskimo arts and crafts, parkas, and bear cubs on display. The Alaska displays proved anti-climactic to us, but it was probably easier to impress visitors who had never been to Alaska.

One of the top attractions, and Phyllis's main interest at the fair, was the Vatican Pavilion's display of Michelangelo's Pietà. However, we children preferred the Sinclair exhibit that included nine life-size Fiberglas dinosaurs, some with moving parts. And U.S. Rubber offered rides (for fifty cents) in an eighty-foot-tall Ferris wheel in the shape of a giant tire.

Glenn's letter home mentioned the futuristic city on display. "It was swingin with cool cars," he wrote.

By the day's end we left the park exhausted and sweaty. The three boys—Jim, Glenn, and Aunt Dot's son Raymond—returned to the car wearing souvenir alpine hats with long feathers. Mom and Phyllis chattered all the way back to Smithtown about the surprise of meeting people they knew at the World's Fair in New York.

The location of the fair, in Flushing Meadows, hosted a previous World's Fair in 1939. A few of the buildings still exist today, and most of the site has been developed into a large park. In fact, completion of the park on that site motivated Robert Moses to hold the fair in 1964/65. Moses, subject of the Pulitzer Prize-winning biography, *The Power Broker* by Robert A. Caro, was determined that the fair should raise enough revenue to finish the infrastructure for the park, left incomplete when the 1939 fair ended in the red.

Moses applied to the Bureau of International Expositions, which sanctions World's Fairs, but due to their prior commitments in 1967 (to Montreal) and 1970 (to Osaka), it denied the application. Moses was miffed, to say the least. His inflammatory remarks about the BIE prompted it to officially discourage member nations from exhibiting in Moses's planned fair.

Not to be dissuaded, Moses gathered many commercial exhibitors, along with those nations, states, and cities that agreed to attend. Many criticized the '64 New York fair for its "crass commercialism," which brought in such exhibits as the giant dinosaurs and the big tire Ferris wheel that thrilled us. Regardless of the criticisms and controversy, Moses completed the Flushing Meadows Park he envisioned, though the event was not an official World's Fair.

Jim spent much of the week hanging out with cousin Raymond, who had a motorcycle but no license. They kept to the back alleys and woods and had a lot of fun together. Jim wrote these observations to his dad: *"You know, I always thought being from New York would be something but these guys don't know so much. Or anyway they sure don't think the same way we do. They sure don't get out and see the world or anything. They think we really know how to live because we're taking this trip, but they are afraid to leave their own places. And they are herded around like sheep. On the streets there are signs to tell you when to walk and when not to walk."*

For Jim, who grew up in a town of a couple of hundred people, with no traffic lights and only one or two stop signs, life on Long Island seemed strange in many ways. Smithtown had more manicured lawns than in all of Alaska—up there we did well to keep the forest from encroaching too close to the house.

I, too, remember being mystified by these relatives who lived only an hour's drive from Manhattan but never visited the city unless absolutely unavoidable. Back in Alaska, my family drove two hours from Anchorage to Moose Pass almost every weekend for years, until the earthquake destroyed the road. I began to realize, like Jim did, that it wasn't where you lived but how you thought about life that made you the person you were.

Phyllis asked Uncle Bill to *"nose around at the airlines for me and find out what kind of jobs they need me for. I definitely like this traveling."* She looked forward to the coming few days at Aunt Betty's house near Washington, D.C., hoping for rest with just one family to visit and not the dozens living on Long Island.

A second letter from Dad reached us in New York. He'd received several of our letters and postcards by June 4, when he wrote the letter from Moose Pass. He wondered how they liked freeway driving, remarked on the rainy weather, talked about his work in Moose Pass and back in Anchorage, where he had hired a family friend to help with the tariff publishing business. Keeping the freight moving at Moose Pass, and the small business running from our house in Anchorage, was turning him into a raving maniac, he claimed. Again he asked where to send his next letter, with no more sign of affection than his closing *Love, Lyle.*

Our week in Smithtown didn't resolve the arguments of twenty years' duration between Mom and Phyllis. In a letter to her dad, Mikie wrote, *Momma and Aunt Winnie had a lot of bets going. One about the bridge at Miller's Pond. Momma says she won and Winnie says she won, so they are still arguing.*

During the week we spent in Smithtown, the Beatles were appointed Members of the British Empire, an honor that prompted one British columnist to complain the state had approved "mindless, ephemeral rubbish," as she called their music. As Beatle-crazy as most teenage girls in America, I thought their new honor was cool. That week the Beatles also first recorded the song "Yesterday," which would become the most covered song in history. Their music provided the soundtrack of my teen years and far beyond.

And the U.S. Senate passed legislation that would require a warning label on all cigarette packs saying: "Caution: Cigarette smoking may be hazardous to your health." Mom tried to quit on the trip, an effort she attempted off and on over many years. She finally succeeded about thirty-five years later, when heart and lung problems threatened her life.

On June 17 we departed Smithtown, heading to see Gram's sister in Queens before touring Manhattan. We rubbernecked our way up Broadway, barely able to absorb all we saw. Smithtown's small-town atmosphere felt very comfortable compared with Manhattan's swarms of people and buildings crammed together in a noisy, chaotic mass. The skyscraper canyons gave way to Central Park and the elaborate historic homes nearby.

A police car pulled up alongside us near Central Park and the officer rolled down his window. "Did yous drive all the way from Alasker with all them crumb-crunchers?" he hollered above the traffic noise.

After a quick reply and a wave, we carried on, winding through the city, craning our necks to see the Empire State Building, the tallest building in the world at that time. In 2019, it had dropped to the world's forty-third tallest, but it is still prominent in the New York skyline, with only two taller buildings. Across the water, we admired the Statue of Liberty, but we had no time to ride out and see her.

Looking for a bridge to take us west into New Jersey, we became disoriented. A nice fellow in a dark alley showed us where to go, according to Mom's diary. None of her letters to Dad mention seeking help from men in dark alleys.

We crossed the bridge in the fading daylight, and looking back, the cityscape resembled a cardboard cutout of lighted buildings against the dark night sky.

Soon we reached our destination, Elizabeth, New Jersey, less than twenty-five miles from Manhattan. That day's travel included the most densely populated and highest traffic territory we had covered. At a motel, we began to relax from the crazy busyness of family visits in Smithtown, the stress of driving in the city, and the freeway traffic with cars whipping around us. Finally, we had just our little band of eight again.

We stopped in New Jersey for Mom. She worked as a tariff specialist for SeaLand Services Inc. in Anchorage, ensuring that SeaLand billed at the correct rate for freight they shipped. Transportation was a man's world at that time, and Mom an exception, working in a position neither clerical nor secretarial. She held fiercely egalitarian views about women in the workforce. Passage of the Equal Pay Act in 1963 delighted her—especially since she worked in an industry dominated by men. Women's rights were prominent in the news, another aspect of the Civil Rights movement.

Mom was eager to meet the staff at SeaLand in New Jersey, people she had become acquainted with through letters and teletype messages.

The people at SeaLand in New Jersey knew her only by her signature on letters, Win Reed. When she arrived at their office June 18 and introduced herself, she was met by shocked stares.

"You're a woman!" someone exclaimed, followed by awkward laughter. Because of her position, they had assumed Win Reed was a man.

Jump forward a few months, and Mom's boss at SeaLand assigned her to train a man, newly hired to work in Mom's department. Bill caught on to the job, and they enjoyed working together.

Then one day—I don't know how the conversation went, exactly—Bill mentioned something about his wages. Mom was stunned to learn that SeaLand paid him significantly more than she earned. She marched into the office of her supervisor, demanding an explanation.

"Win, you know he has a family to support."

"We are doing the same job, and I have more experience!"

"But Win, you have a husband to support you."

With the courage of her convictions, Mom terminated her employment at SeaLand. In her early thirties, she lacked the confidence to sue the company in court over the issue, as she could, citing the Equal Pay Act. And she may not have had Dad's support to take legal action that might affect his own standing in the transportation community. But she wouldn't just sit back and accept their unfair treatment.

Equality and justice were always important to Mom, and although not politically involved, she championed those values in everyday life.

Dad, too, went to bat for us. He usually approached issues with more pragmatism than principle. A couple of years later, our school dress codes required Marlie and me to wear dresses or skirts, despite the daily wait at our bus stop in freezing weather. On one below-zero day, Dad insisted we wear pants to school. Our teachers sent us to the office, where the principal called Dad to remind him of the requirements: if we wore pants, we had to bring a dress or skirt to change into at school.

Dad wrote to the school leaders, berating the hardships created by requiring either waiting for the bus wearing a dress, or buying us a bigger wardrobe, one he couldn't afford. They ultimately changed the policy, so in cold weather we could wear pants to school.

After her resignation from SeaLand, Mom soon found another job, and a year or so later, Dad's employer moved our family to Nikiski, a nearly four-hour drive south of Anchorage, on the Kenai Peninsula. There we discovered that her SeaLand trainee, Bill, had moved to Kenai, just a few miles south of us. He hired Mom to work for him in a travel agency.

Mom loved the travel business, and in the early 1970s she had moved back to Anchorage and worked for another travel agency. Every stereotype of 1960s male sexism applied to the owners of that agency, and their employment practices included suggestive "compliments" and a hands-on approach to female employees. I worked there myself for about six months during a break from college.

By that time, my parents had separated, and Mom stood up for herself. She worked to unionize the travel agency staff, and lost her job over it. The National Labor Relations Board investigated, and that particular "good ole boys" club was forced to change its ways. By the conclusion of the lawsuit, she had found a better job with the airlines, and another travel agency hired me when I graduated from University of Alaska.

Back to 1965 in Elizabeth, New Jersey, Mom laughed at the confusion in the SeaLand office, their thinking "Win" was a man, and she toured the operations and ate lunch with some of her colleagues. SeaLand had revolutionized the shipping industry in 1956 (when the company was known as Pan-Atlantic) with the introduction of uniform shipping containers—those same containers that now fill shipping ports and freight terminals around the world.

The rest of us cleaned up the car and rested at the motel. After lunch, we picked up Mom and continued south to Virginia and Aunt Betty's house. I bemoaned the many historic locations we passed by, like Philadelphia and the Liberty Bell, and Valley Forge. But we had a lot more ground to cover before we returned to Alaska.

I found a Time Magazine at the motel and read about the U.S. troop buildup in South Vietnam and bombing raids being carried out there. The Committee for Non-Violent Action (CNVA) launched a "summer of protest" against U.S. policies in Vietnam with a "speak-in" at the Pentagon. About 200 CNVA supporters demonstrated and spoke in favor of peaceful alternatives, and handed out some 60,000 leaflets to Pentagon personnel. They called for the resignations of Secretary of State Dean Rusk, presidential advisor McGeorge Bundy, and Defense Secretary Robert McNamara. According to Gallup polls in 1965, public support for government policies was above 60 percent. But the organized opposition made itself heard.

Newspapers published a photo of Patricia Anne Morgan, a twenty-six-year-old model, who was summoned to court because of the shorts she wore in New York City's Riverside Park. The court determined that the length of her shorts did not actually violate the statute, but the judge advised her against wearing them anyway. Her shorts were very similar to those Mom wore for much of the trip. I never imagined Mom risked arrest, but I'm sure she would have considered it just another adventure.

Chapter 10

THE REUNION OF THE THREE SISTERS, late on a hot June night, erupted into a frenzy of hugs and tears and exclamations.

"Look at these kids!"

"What took you so long to get here?"

"Look at Jim! He's taller than Frank!"

"Mama! Give me a hug!"

The scene Mom and Phyllis imagined when they first envisioned our trip played out on that Virginia summer evening.

Aunt Betty and her husband, Frank, had left Alaska in 1957. Betty and her siblings wrote letters back and forth, but mail sometimes took weeks to reach Alaska, delivered to the state by truck or ship unless we paid a premium for air mail service. When the Alaskan family members gathered at Christmas, they usually placed one phone call to Betty, with each of her six siblings taking a turn to say, "Merry Christmas, Betty! How are you? How are the kids?"

or some hurried variation on that theme. Those calls, brief and expensive, usually proved unsatisfying.

We spent a week at Betty's house, suffering heat in the nineties and high humidity with no air conditioning. On many days, we explored: the Capitol building, wax museum, Mount Vernon, the National Archives, the mint, and the Smithsonian.

My love of history devoured a gourmet diet that week. I could have spent the whole week at the Smithsonian.

"Look at this!" I called to Marlie in the Museum of Health and Medicine. "It says the person had elephantiasis," I said, reading from the nearby label.

Marlie stared briefly at the swollen leg, preserved in a large jar, then glanced along the shelf where additional jars offered brains, or diseased livers, or amputated tumors. She wilted, swallowed hard, and headed for the door.

The medical displays fascinated me, but so did the natural history, air and space displays, and the trove of history.

Mom wrote to Dad about our visit to the National Archives: *"You'd have loved the Archives building. Has all the old original manuscripts and papers of the country—Declaration of Independence, Bill of Rights, etc. Original letters of George Washington and other famouses. 'Hawk-Eye' (Sandy) spotted the treaty we signed with Russia when Alaska was purchased, (all written in Russian, of course)."*

At Arlington National Cemetery we visited President Kennedy's grave and the Tomb of the Unknown Soldier. The ceremonious marching of the guards and the acres of white crosses put us all in a somber mood, and I thought of my dad's uncle, Everett Reed, who had died in World War II.

"Do you think he's buried here?" I asked.

Mom thought he might be, and we searched for his name on a cross until the size of the place overwhelmed us.

Many years later we learned that Everett was buried in Europe, and Glenn finally found his name on a white cross at the American Cemetery in Luxembourg a couple of years ago. He died crossing the Rhine, only weeks before the Allies claimed victory in Europe. He earned a posthumous Silver Star for heroism, having lost his life while helping the other men from his boat to safety.

Aunt Betty and Uncle Frank drove a station wagon, and one day all thirteen of us piled into it to go swimming at Lake Fairfax. On the way back we stopped at a drive-in, the kind where you drove up to a parking spot with a telephone mounted on a pole, along with a poster of the menu. From that phone, you placed your order and a carhop brought your food to the car.

To avoid chaos (a dim hope at best), we examined the menu and organized our order before soft-spoken Uncle Frank picked up the phone.

"May I take your order?" a voice blared.

"Yes," he began. "We need four Mighty Mos, two half fried chickens, two teen twists, five orders of onion rings, three French fries, one hot dog, two vanilla milkshakes, one quarter chicken, one strawberry milkshake, two cheeseburgers, one barbecue chicken, one milk, two Cokes, three iced teas, and two double-dip sodas. And please include some napkins."

After a pause, the waiter said, "Will that be all, sir?"
"Yes, that's all."

"I should hope so, sir."

As we waited, still crammed into the station wagon, one of us had to use the bathroom. This started a chain reaction, and ten of us trooped off to the restrooms. Of course, this took time.

The carhop arrived with two heaping trays. When he saw only Frank, Betty, and Gram in the car, he frowned, then checked the sales ticket on one of the trays.

"Is this your order, sir?"

"Yes, that's for us," Frank said, reaching for the food.

The rest of us had a good view of the carhop's shock and confusion as he handed in the great mound of food and collected payment. He walked away shaking his head.

An original note includes the prices for our order, which totaled $12.44. Those were the days of forty-five-cent cheeseburgers, fifteen-cent Cokes, and twenty-five-cent French fries.

In spite of all the fun, I still had my mind on school. In a letter to Dad, I begged him (yelling in all capital letters) to send my grades as soon as possible. None of the other kids cared a bit about theirs, but I loved school and valued the affirmation of a good report card.

Marlie had saved her weekly allowance for a few weeks, and during our stay at Aunt Betty's house, she spent $2.99 to buy a pack of fifty-seven different fireworks. One evening she set up a fireworks display in the street for us and started setting them off.

When one of them flared enough to light up the block, the street light, which had come on automatically at dusk, went dark.

Marlie looked up, fear and guilt mingling in her shocked expression. What had she done? Was she in trouble?

Mom explained to her that the streetlights were controlled automatically by the light, to Marlie's great relief.

She wrote to Dad the next day: *"The Shower of Pearls was so brite that it put out the street light across the street!"*

At the zoo, we stared long and hard at a gorilla smoking a cigarette. I suspect Marlie's fascination with monkeys and apes began with that gorilla—the first she ever saw; she still giggles like her eleven-year-old self when she sees them in a zoo. The size of rhinos and hippos impressed Glenn, who told Dad the zoo was a blast. *The jirafts are as tall as the brees in the trees,* he wrote. Zoos of the 1960s seldom offered the naturalistic environments seen today. Lions, tigers, bears, and apes prowled small enclosures of concrete with strong fencing. We saw many animals in a short time but felt sorry for them in their cramped cages.

Before we left town, we saw the film *Mary Poppins*. We savored the fun and fantasy of it and drove around the rest of the country singing tunes from the show. Family tradition required that we write new lyrics for those songs, and we did so, describing our travels.

A week sped by, and our day of departure arrived, time to leave Betty and her family behind.

One of Mom's letters says: *"If it were to suddenly become necessary for us to go home without seeing another person or sight, this trip would be worth it anyway just to relive the joy on Betty's face when we got here."* Betty missed her family in Alaska so much, she wanted us to stay for two weeks. But as always, more sights to see awaited down the road.

Mom may have been satisfied to end the trip there, but I certainly wasn't. What about the rest of our plans—Mexico and the Grand Canyon and Disneyland? As we packed the van on June 27—including about two hundred pounds more gear than we arrived with, by Mom's estimation—I felt reassured knowing we would not return to Alaska, not yet. Our Wayward Bus headed down the East Coast for our first encounter with the Deep South.

On June 28, the day we left Virginia, Jim worked up the gumption to write a letter to Uncle Bill, one which weighed on him for five thousand miles. *I have something to admit,* he wrote. *this is pretty chicken of me to tell you now where you can't kick my but but anyway in my room under the picture of the Jaguar (s type) is a whole in the wall. I put it there with a basketball about 3 days before I left. I haven't told mom. I am sorry about it but it is done. I have inclosed $20.00 of my money to get it fixed. Now I feel better. Love, Jim*

I suspect Jim talked to my mom about this, even if he didn't talk to his own. Mom shared a close relationship with Jim, as she did with many of her nieces and nephews, and later with her grandchildren. Well into adulthood, Jim occasionally called her to talk about his troubles. When she owned a travel agency, he persuaded her to front him an airline ticket if he was short of money. In the 1990s, while browsing in her friend's bookstore, Mom glanced out at an eighteen-wheeler stopped for a red light. She recognized Jim at the wheel. Without a word to her friend, she raced out the door, climbed up to the cab, and leapt into the passenger seat before the light changed. Her friend thought she had lost her mind, but after having lunch with Jim, Mom returned and explained her hasty departure.

At Betty's house we caught up on news of the wider world. Divers brought up the first treasures from a Spanish galleon discovered a thousand feet off the coast of Florida, part of a 1715 Treasure Fleet sunk in a hurricane.

In Pennsylvania, four golfers were killed and six injured when lightning struck a shed where they sought refuge during a rainstorm. Lightning storms, the game of golf, and the state of Pennsylvania were equally foreign to me.

And twenty-seven B-52 Stratofortress bombers began flying regular missions from Guam to North Vietnam. More than seven hundred of the planes built for the military had been delivered in June 1955, almost exactly ten years before their first bombing mission. An article in the *Kansas City (Missouri) Times* in June 1965 said the military expected to continue use of the B-52 fleet into the 1970s. Remarkably, many B-52s are still in service today, and a 2018 article in *Popular Mechanics* cited indications that as the Air Force continues to modify and modernize them, they could be flying in 2050. A future pilot may fly the same plane his or her great-grandfather flew.

Chapter 11

BEFORE WE LEFT VIRGINIA, Mom received a long letter from Dad written June 21. He'd driven from Moose Pass to Anchorage the day before, their first sunny day in a month. Snow continued to accumulate in the mountains around Moose Pass well into June. He mentioned his work, a few friends he'd seen, and trouble finding a tenant for their rental house in Anchorage. He'd traded in his car for a blue 1965 Chevy pickup and loved the way it drove, except on gravel roads—which still existed in long stretches on the Seward Highway. *It's a little light in the rear end dept. But then I have the same problem.* I don't know what compelled him to add *I've been vigorously persuing girls with an amazing lack of success.* He continued with news of a friend's death, fisticuffs breaking out at the Anchorage City Council meeting, and the sighting of a tiny moose calf as they loaded freight in Moose Pass. Someone caught the motherless baby moose and was *trying to get the Fish*

& Game chaps to come and get it. Couldn't get it to take any milk. Sure was small.

Sounds like you had a ball at the fair and are enjoying the trip, he said in closing. *Sometimes I wish I were along, but it just can't be I guess.*

That was his longest and newsiest letter of the summer.

We found our way to the house of Mom and Phyllis's cousin Honey in North Carolina. A cornfield nearly surrounded the place.

It's hard now to imagine a cornfield as something exotic, but we had never seen corn growing before. Agriculture in Alaska was limited, to say the least. Yes, the long daylight hours allow some vegetables to grow very large during the limited growing season, averaging 105 days. Hundred-pound cabbages and fifteen-pound carrots grow in the Matanuska Valley north of Anchorage. But corn requires a level of heat in the soil and air that Alaska rarely achieves.

Mom raised a garden wherever we lived, but our summer gardens held what most of the country considers winter crops, or at least cool season crops. The exceptions are very fast-growing greens—spinach and lettuce, green onions, and radishes. Not corn.

In one of her letters, Mom described Aunt Betty's garden in Virginia for Dad.

"Betty has 2 apple trees and a grape arbor in her back yard ... and a garden with tomatoes and corn and impossible things like that."

When we piled out of the van at Cousin Honey's house late in the afternoon June 28, I wanted a closer look at the cornfield growing right alongside the strip of lawn next to her house. We kids all needed to stretch and run around the yard after a day on the road, and we ended up along the cornfield, peering down the rows as the shadows lengthened.

Meanwhile, Mom and Phyllis and Honey hugged and chatted. Honey was about six years old when Mom's family left New York, but their families had been close. Cousins in New York phoned Honey after our visit there a couple of weeks earlier, and she welcomed us eagerly.

"You kids go pick us some corn for supper." Honey made our day with that request.

The younger kids disappeared into the rows of corn, while I cautiously stepped into the dim yellow-green shade. The largest tasseled ears were probably the best, I assumed, but I had never picked one before. What if the whole cornstalk broke? Could you just pull them off at random, or should all the ears be taken off a stalk at one picking? My ignorance of corn knew no bounds. Finally I reached for a big ear, determined to try pulling it off.

A flash of motion a few inches from my face prompted me to jump back. A spider darted away as I brushed against his web. Suddenly I became aware of the insect sounds around me—the rattle of cicadas in the trees, the grinding hum of June bugs. My bare feet in the warm soil might be close to some creeping thing, and I shuddered right down to my toes. I wanted to shrink away and escape like a wisp of breeze. Who knew how scary a cornfield could be?

I crept to the edge of the field. The other kids carried loads of corn. I screwed up my courage and grabbed a couple of nearby ears. As we gathered on the porch, I glanced around for bugs, knowing they would be flying toward the porch light as darkness fell.

"Can we go back out and play in the corn?" Marlie, Mikie, and Glenn actually enjoyed it.

"You can help shuck this corn," Mom said.

"I'll help," I volunteered, jumping onto the porch. At least I could run inside quickly if I needed to. Gram and I set to work, and Mom said the little kids could go play.

Honey called after them as they raced across the lawn. "Don't go too far into the cornfield. And watch out for snakes!"

Snakes? Why didn't she think to mention that when we first ventured out there? The evening air was warm, but I shivered, more glad than ever to shuck corn on the porch.

Gram and I grabbed an ear each and pulled at the corn husks, eventually peeling them down to mostly bare ears of corn. Back in Alaska, corn arrived in cans, and the rare fresh corn at the store cost too much for us. As Gram instructed me in corn shucking, corn silk littered the porch and our laps. Gaining confidence, I chose another ear and pulled the husks down on one side.

Gram did the same then held her ear of corn out toward me. "Look at that."

There, a fat gray caterpillar munched away among the yellow kernels. Gram just brushed it away.

Now another anxiety jolted my heart rate and slowed my fingers. I didn't want to smash a caterpillar into the corn.

Eventually we ate supper, juice from the buttery sweet corn dripping down our chins. The temperature dropped a few degrees—never enough for us—and we spread into every spare corner of Honey's house to sleep. Visions of spiders and snakes danced in my head.

Out in the world, the *High Point (North Carolina) Enterprise* reported inauguration of commercial satellite phone service, kicked off by a transatlantic call placed by President Johnson, and quickly followed with similar calls by officials in Canada, France, England, Germany, and Italy. The calls were relayed by the Early Bird satellite, launched into orbit by a joint venture of forty-four countries. The call quality was clear, and similar to earlier calls which used undersea cables across the Atlantic. Voices bouncing to another country via a satellite in space seemed like science fiction coming true. I stared at the feeble stars and wondered how it could possibly work.

Headlines that week also mentioned the campaign of propaganda leaflets—along with bombs—being dropped on North Vietnam. The leaflets claimed that Vietnamese rice supplies were being traded in China for military hardware. Leaflets were used to threaten bombings, reduce morale, and sometimes provide health and hygiene information. Reward leaflets also offered money for the return of servicemen's remains, for intelligence, and for military hardware. In June 1965 alone, planes dropped 4.8 million leaflets, and in the course of the war, billions of leaflets littered North and South Vietnam.

The propaganda flew both ways. North Vietnam dropped leaflets intended to demoralize American troops. Recognizing the racial tensions in the U.S., some carried the message that in America, blacks were sent to the back of the line but overseas, America's military sent black servicemen to the front lines. Others cited the spreading opposition back home to U.S. presence in Vietnam.

Regardless of leaflets, the war raged on. Guerillas shot down a C-123 cargo plane thirteen miles from

Saigon, with conflicting reports citing sixteen or twenty dead.

We left Honey's house the next day with a gunnysack stuffed with corn, at least a hundred ears. After eating corn every day, and giving some away, we finally emptied the gunnysack somewhere along the Gulf of Mexico.

Chapter 12

HIGHWAY 17 RAN DOWN NEAR THE COAST of Georgia, and people along the way told us it would be cooler if we kept closer to the ocean.

"Maybe it is, compared with the Sahara Desert," Phyllis quipped.

In a letter to Dad, Mom wrote: *"We are about to perish in this heat—no lie."* From our home in Alaska, under a blanket of snow the previous winter, the sunny south had sounded so appealing. Now we were miserable and sweaty, with nothing to distract us from the heat. Nothing but poverty.

Along the road in Georgia, we happened on a row of stands, dotted a few yards apart for several miles, with black women weaving baskets or fanning themselves in the shade of a flimsy shed. Children in rags played nearby. Occasionally a toothless old man sat with them. Some offered watermelons or corn for sale, but the baskets drew us in.

Despite our overloaded van, Mom and Phyllis decided to stop and look. We could use the baskets as gifts for the relatives we planned to visit in Florida, they reasoned. We pulled up to a stand where an elderly black woman stood. She watched with rheumy eyes as we approached and examined her expert weaving.

The realization crept over me that she depended on this roadside stand, her entire livelihood. Her tattered dress and weary stance spoke of hardships and cares I could not imagine. Had she only ever woven baskets along this poor stretch of road for a few dollars?

Marlie, always more forthright than I, asked her how old she was. Her blank stare suggested that she rarely thought of the matter. At last she said she didn't remember. We could only guess that she was around ninety. Old enough that her parents may even have been enslaved on one of the plantations in the area.

Phyllis and Gram chose some baskets, and the woman lifted one and then another from her supply, pushing each toward us. "This one?" she asked. "You like this one?" Our limited space in the van meant nothing to her.

We loaded up our few purchases, and as we prepared to pull away, she approached the car window. Peering inside, she said, "You got somethin' to eat?" She had no food and couldn't leave her stand all day. "Candy bar? Got any candy bars?" she pleaded. We gathered up all the prepared food in our cooler—a peanut butter sandwich left from lunch, a banana, and a slice of cantaloupe.

As tears of gratitude rolled down her wrinkled cheeks, we sped away with lumps in our throats. The oppressive heat took second place to the oppressive poverty surrounding us along the road: people living in patched-together shacks with no hope for a future, only that someone would buy a basket or melon so their kids could eat a meager supper. Poor white people lived along those roads too. They sat on the sagging porches of houses with peeling paint, fanning themselves with their hats as we drove past.

As we tooled along toward Florida, nobody said much. The spirit of our supercalifragilisticexpialidocious journey retreated as we contemplated the poor people, both black and white, who lived in circumstances we could not fathom. Questions swirled in my mind that I could find no words to express, stranger that I was in that strange land.

Alaska's population in the 1960s included few black residents outside the military. The military bases were across town from us, on the northeast side of the city. In my elementary school years, I can recall only one black classmate. I wonder now if she felt as much a stranger in Alaska as I did that day in Georgia.

Our family wasn't wealthy. For three years, we lived in a small house in Anchorage built by my dad and uncles as an addition to a tractor garage. After that we bought a place south of town, only an unfinished basement, waiting for the house we hoped to build on top. But an oil heater kept us warm, and plumbing worked in the kitchen and bathroom. The basement walls rose a couple of feet above ground level, and the flat roof—which would become the floor of the first story, we hoped, was sheathed with tarpaper and hot-mopped with tar to seal it. Dad planned to build the house on top during weekends and long summer evenings. Concrete stairs, with their own slanted roof and walls to keep off the snow, led down to our front door. A similar enclosed stairway led to a back door. Marlie, Glenn, and I slept on triple bunk beds, and a curtain hung in place of a bathroom door. Dad hunted sheep or goat to stock the freezer.

By the time we moved again, Dad had framed in the upstairs, but it still needed wiring, plumbing, and insulation.

Alaska abounded with run-down houses, and with people who survived on their resourcefulness. But the people along Highway 17 barely survived, and many seemed beyond hope. The facts of poverty and racism gave way to the truths that people with influence and means rarely acted on behalf of the vulnerable and disenfranchised. A few did. Would I? At thirteen I did not see myself as a person of influence.

In Georgia I began to see why people would march to the capitol, facing armed police, firehoses, and gunfire, to gain some hope of equality in education and jobs, of freedom to use public buses and bathrooms. What did they have to lose? Precious little.

Marlie was indignant. What kind of country tolerated this level of poverty? She expressed her outrage in a letter to President Johnson, but Marlie's copy of the letter has been lost.

Mom wrote this to Dad: *"These are the lessons that you can't learn from books! We have been hearing things now and then about the racial strife and have been holding our tongues as you guys warned, but it is hard to do and it certainly goes against the grain to be afraid to express our opinion on civil equality in this 'free' country of ours. Even a few of our relatives have prejudices we would never have believed. Mikie shocked the daylights out of a couple of relatives the other night by speaking her mind in rebuttal to a derogatory remark about Negroes when she spouted, "My Grandpa taught me that 'God made the little Negro and he made him in the night, and he made him in a hurry and forgot to paint him white' ... and that's the only difference!" With that she turned on her heel and stomped outdoors."*

Of course, today Mikie's impassioned defense is considered derogatory.

Mom's letter continued: *"Perhaps we don't really know much about the 'cause' of the American Negro, for instance, but we do know that those Negroes who are rebelling, have a goal—they, at least, are doing something about a thing they believe in! And who the hell are we to say they are going about it the wrong way? We've never had to fight for anything!"*

Dad and Uncle Bill, and a few other friends, had warned us to keep our ideas to ourselves as we traveled through the South. Opportunities abounded to bite our tongues—at gas stations, campgrounds, restaurants—so many places with bathrooms marked "whites only" and where black men were called "boy" regardless of any legal requirements for equality.

On we drove, trying to figure things out along the way, our minds whirling with new experiences and ideas. Whatever influence we thought of exercising was effectively silenced by those warnings. Those who warned us intended the warnings to help us avoid racial hostilities and violence like we'd seen on television over issues we didn't understand.

I began to see risks associated with being a voice for good in the world.

Those speaking up for civil rights certainly faced those risks, and sometimes gave their lives. Black activists were accused of promoting Communism and being under the control of Communists. Dr. Martin Luther King Jr., the most visible, spoke publicly around the country and received death threats on a regular basis. He and others risked—and experienced—arrest and imprisonment for civil disobedience to desegregate schools, register black voters, and promote equality in employment and justice before the law. After driving along Highway 17 in Georgia, we began to see why he would risk so much. For King, the risks ended with his assassination in 1968, but others continued to pursue the dreams he spoke of so eloquently in 1963.

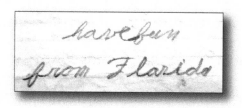

Chapter 13

LATE THAT DAY we crossed the state line into Florida and camped at Fort Clinch State Park on Amelia Island. In addition to the old fort, the entry to Cumberland Sound featured lots of beach. Sounded ideal but smelled like rotten eggs! The sulfur odor is forever imprinted in my mind as the stink of Florida. We were dying to cool off in the ocean, but signs marked the beaches off-limits due to dangerous currents. More signs warned of alligators in some areas, effectively dampening our desire to swim.

The Spanish first fortified the spot in the early 1700s. I imagined their galleons off the coast and wondered if the treasure ship I'd heard about on the news had sunk nearby.

After almost two hundred years of intermittent military use, including the Seminole wars, the Civil War, and the Spanish-American War, the fort was abandoned. It deteriorated until the 1930s when the Civilian Conservation Corps began a restoration project. In 1935 the State of Florida bought the property and surrounding 235 acres and turned it into Fort Clinch State Park. A play celebrating the area's history, "Romance of the Eight Flags," was advertised but wouldn't be performed until a couple of weeks later.

We wandered the water's edge, wary of 'gators but wishing we could cool off. To the west, the St. Mary's River divided into countless swampy channels as it sought the sea. We explored the fort at the very northern tip of Florida and the Atlantic coast to the east. Finally we crawled into the van for the night.

The following morning, July 1, we drove to St. Augustine, and consumed a further dose of history. After seeing the oldest house and the oldest store in North America, we visited the Ripley's Believe it or Not Museum.

I ogled Ripley's wonders: the four-thousand-year-old mummy, freaks of nature like the two-headed calf, and a postage-stamp-sized paper containing the whole Constitution. In a note to my dad, I joked, *"I thought I recognized one of the shrunken heads, but it turned out to be a Zulu chief, so I was wrong."* After we squirmed and grimaced at the morbidly fascinating exhibits, an attendant gave us paper cups of fresh-squeezed orange juice. Free!

The marvel of it may be lost on people who never lived far from sources of fresh produce, much less such a tropical delight as fresh orange juice. I grew up thinking Tang and orange juice were pretty much the same. Now I knew fresh-squeezed orange juice tasted wonderful and very different than anything I'd consumed in Alaska.

Throughout the summer I experienced many kinds of real, fresh food for the first time. And in Florida, a lot of it was fruit. The cost of shipping produce to Alaska made watermelon a once-a-year treat and pineapple even rarer. After all, pineapple could be bought in a can, like so many of our foods. I did not eat fresh asparagus until well into adulthood.

We occasionally grew tomatoes in Alaska but not in any quantity. The "fresh" tomatoes we bought in the store were packed somewhere in the Lower 48, and they ripened on their way to Alaska in a shipping container. Low on flavor, with a plasticky surface appearance, they bore limited resemblance to the delicious red fruit that makes vine-ripened tomatoes so popular.

Now, as we drove around the country through the summer growing season, we experienced the real flavor of fresh foods. And with fresh-squeezed orange juice free, we knew we were living large.

Two of Gram's brothers, and one of my late grandpa's sisters, lived in Florida, and we stopped to visit each of them. We kept our road atlas handy, but the maps lacked detail. We needed more specific directions to their houses.

"We're only an hour or so away," Mom said. "Let's call them for directions before we drive much closer."

Phyllis wheeled the car off the main road north of West Palm Beach. "Hey, kids, help us find a pay phone."

Almost all gas stations had a pay phone out front. Phyllis dialed, and when Uncle Sal answered, she jotted down the directions and handed her notes to Mom. Soon we returned to the road, looking for a crossroad called Highway 98.

"There it is!" one of us shouted from the back.

"I see it now," Phyllis said.

"Do we turn here, or is it just a landmark for us?" Mom frowned at the notes.

"Straight past it, I think. What's the next thing?"

"After that it says 'three miles to Four Points.' Is that another town?"

"He didn't say," Phyllis said.

We allowed for human error and made a couple of swags (scientific wild-ass guesses) and drove another couple of miles. Fearing we'd gone too far, Phyllis set us all looking for another pay phone. Pay phones, thin on the ground now, appeared frequently in the landscape of 1965.

When we found one, we called again.

Phyllis wrote later, *"Uncle Sal got all excited and said we had gone too far and to go back to the light at the intersection (four points—good grief!) and wait for him, or rather he'd be waiting for us. So we drove back, crossed the intersection and waited at a diagonal from where we thought we should be because there was a place to park right in front of a bank with a big night light that would shine on us. We waited for 15 or 20 minutes, then called again. This sent Aunt Mary into a panic and it was a good thing her brother was there because Uncle Sal had gone looking for us. So Aunt Mary's brother took charge and we described where we were which was just a few blocks from them so we were to stay right there and he'd be right over. In the meantime a cop pulled up behind us and we thought, "Oh God, now we'll have to move and everyone will be out looking all over the state for us." The cop came over and asked if we were relatives of Sal Arcuri, and we said yes. He pointed to where we had been originally and said, "Your uncle is over there waiting for you!"*

I value the convenience of smart phones, with their GPS and map capabilities, but I never lost my love of paper maps, which began during that summer's odyssey. Paper maps are becoming a thing of the past, but I much prefer the broad perspective they offer to the tiny slice of map on my cell phone screen. For one thing, a big map reveals places along my route that are worth a side trip, places I would never find on my smart phone. There's no sense of adventure or exploration using GPS, just the turn-by-turn routing from one point to another.

Our visit with Gram's brothers, Sal and Nick, exposed us to more Florida fun—and sun. Aunt Mary's sister Ann took us to the beach. Ann reminded me of a beach ball with stick legs and arms. She didn't mind making a scene and floated on her back in the ocean, singing at the top of her lungs. Such was the price of our trip to the beach, though we tried to ignore her.

Under that intense Florida sun, we baked. Our faces, shoulders, backs, and legs roasted to a rosy hue, painful when we moved. It hurt to remove our clothes that night. Even my scalp hurt where a line of sunburn marked the part in my hair. Mom applied every sort of salve and cream to ease our pain enough to sleep, but mostly in vain.

The next morning Uncle Sal picked mangos from a tree in his backyard for our breakfast—without a doubt my first taste of a fruit that is one of my favorites.

Mom and Phyl didn't want to be on the road during the holiday weekend, so we stayed and watched fireworks in West Palm Beach on the Fourth of July, something of a novelty to watch them in the dark. In southcentral Alaska, early July nights are bright as day until almost 11 p.m., when twilight sets in for a couple of hours. Up there, if you want fireworks in the dark, you stay up until midnight— or save them for New Year's Eve.

We drove from West Palm Beach to Hollywood, Florida, to visit with Gram's brother Nick and his wife. They served us a long, relaxed, and typically Italian lasagna dinner, and we visited all day, careful to avoid the sun this time. My letters rarely spoke of our meals, but in a letter to Dad I mentioned that all-day dinner, along with another reminder to send my grades.

Mom and Phyllis wanted to drive on across Florida to Port Charlotte, where we would visit their Aunt Lillian and Uncle Bill Arns. Darkness began to fall, but they still wanted to travel across Florida through the Everglades. Phyllis had called Aunt Lillian earlier in the day and learned that she was holding some mail for us—a strong motivation to push on.

Uncle Sal said we shouldn't drive on the Tamiami Trail at night.

Uncle Nick told us snakes and panthers roamed the Everglades. Alligators awaited us in the canals right along the road.

Aunt Mary shuddered as she warned us of the bugs.

Not to be deterred, we loaded up the van, and at about ten o'clock, Uncle Nick led us to the edge of town, and the beginning of the Tamiami Trail.

Work crews pushed this road through the nearly impenetrable swampland of south Florida fewer than forty years earlier, with two lanes and a watery wilderness for miles on either side. No moon shone down to temper the blackness of that steaming hot night. We stared silently, seeing nothing beyond the headlights. Thunder rumbled. A sheet of lightning lit the road ahead of us, illuminating the eerie cypress trees whose mossy arms groped toward us from the surrounding swamp.

As we forged through the quagmire, insects, drawn to our headlights, smashed against our windshield, leaving green smears in the arc of the wiper blades. The noise of the lightning storm—totally alien to our Alaskan experience—and the insects flying at us magnified the fears instilled in us by the uncles. Tensions inside our van rose by the minute.

Phyllis's narrative added this: *"As we rounded a curve, a sign loomed up proclaiming 'INDIAN VILLAGE.' "What Indians?" "Must be Seminoles." My mind raced back through the years frantically grasping at forgotten shreds of information on American Indians. All I could remember from my 6th grade history about the Seminoles was that they were particularly vicious and had never signed a treaty with the whites.*

"Now there were Indians behind the cypress trees, their arrow heads glinting with each new bolt of lightning."

Mom and Phyllis debated whether to turn back, but after checking the mileage, found we passed the halfway point already. On we ventured, with Mom at the wheel, white-knuckled and determined to bring us through safely.

A sudden wobbling sensation and clunking noise stood our hairs on end. A flat tire!

My cousin Jim, the "man of the house," groaned loudly. He pushed open the side door and stepped into the steaming darkness. "I can't even see out here."

Mom climbed down from the driver's seat to hold a flashlight, but had to put her long pajama bottoms on to keep the bugs off. She sprayed Jim down with bug dope with her free hand as he changed the tire.

They managed to evade death at the hands—or jaws—of the snakes and 'gators, and we arrived safely, though a little worse for wear, in Port Charlotte at 2 a.m.

Our tribe of eight more than filled Aunt Lillian and her husband Bill's house. (Lillian was my late Grandpa Sanders' sister.) Fortunately, Grandpa's cousin Leola also lived in Port Charlotte, and Mom stayed at Leola's house with a couple of us kids to spread out the hosting duties.

We remembered tales of Leola from Gram's stories of the olden days. While they were schoolchildren in New York, she was Gram's neighbor and best friend, and they had been cheerleaders together. When she fell in love with Leola's cousin Phil, Gram's Italian family sabotaged their wedding even after Phil completed all the classes to become a Roman Catholic. Leola helped them elope in a taxi, chased across Long Island by Gram's brothers. The taxi driver stopped at a friend's house—he'd promised to teach him to milk his cow. Fortunately, when the taxi driver pulled in to his friend's yard for the milking lesson, Gram's brothers lost their trail.

A week into July, we left Port Charlotte and drove north up the west coast of Florida. Most of our family visits were completed. But friends up the road near New Orleans, and some in Texas, awaited our arrival.

Out in the world that week, Trigger, the beloved horse of Roy Rogers, featured in more than eighty films and television episodes, died at thirty-three years old. Rogers arranged for a taxidermist to preserve Trigger, rearing on his hind legs, and displayed him for many years in the Roy Rogers and Dale Evans Museum, first in Victorville, California, and later in Branson, Missouri. After the museum closed in 2009, RFD-TV, a network featuring rural and western programming, bought Trigger for more than a quarter million dollars.

And on July 4, President Johnson sat at a desk in front of the Statue of Liberty and signed the Immigration and Nationality Act of 1965, abolishing a nationality-based immigration quota system in place since 1921. Quotas remained in the new act, divided only between eastern and western hemispheres, and preference was given to immigrants with skills needed in the American workforce. Emphasis was placed on reuniting families. Later immigration changes, in the 1980s, added refugees as a special category but did not increase overall immigration quotas.

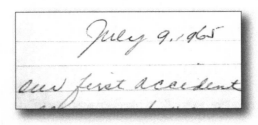

July 9, 1965

our first accident

Chapter 14

Although I knew little about Cuba in 1965 (and, sadly, don't know much more now), I had heard of the "communist threat" to our nation from that island. On this subject, Mom and Uncle Bill disagreed loudly. Uncle Bill, as a civil defense leader in Moose Pass, met regularly with a small band of men to plan for our protection from the Reds. While they sat around Phyllis's table drinking black coffee and tallying the defensive resources of Moose Pass, Mom listened from the next room, scoffing at their efforts as fantasies born of paranoia. Who in their right mind would attack Moose Pass, Alaska, and for what possible end?

After one such meeting, Mom muttered, in Uncle Bill's hearing, "I won't waste any time and money building bomb shelters."

"Better minds than yours are coming up with these plans, Winnie," Bill shot back.

"Says you! I'll take my chances."

"You'll do more than that," Bill yelled. He grabbed

his civil defense notebook and shook it in her direction. "If there's an attack I have the authority to shoot anyone who doesn't cooperate—"

Phyllis grabbed his arm, screaming. "You'd shoot my sister?"

It was probably just as well our family moved to Anchorage in 1957, before war broke out between Mom and Bill.

During the Cold War, in the 1950s, American-backed leaders in Cuba were routed, and many fled to exile in Florida, a hundred miles away. By 1960, Fidel Castro rose to power and allied himself with the Soviet Union.

The Cuban exiles in America, with the help of the CIA and Cuban counter-revolutionaries, formed a military force that invaded Cuba in April 1961. This attempted invasion, at the Bay of Pigs on the island's southern coast, proved a complete failure.

A major outcome: Castro gained hero status in his country and strengthened his ties with the Soviet Union. America's Cold War anxieties ramped up, even as far away as Alaska. I would have been hard-pressed to find the Bay of Pigs on a map, but my own anxieties rose over talk of Castro, the failed invasion, and the eventual result, the Cuban Missile Crisis. Was the threat real or imagined? By 1965 these events were a couple of years behind us, but we knew Florida was the closest to Cuba we would be.

As we drove up Florida's sweltering Gulf Coast, we found a state park where we could camp. We rolled out our van's side tent and set up the aluminum loungers. Following our well-established routine, we quickly located the campground showers and greeted our neighboring campers while Mom and Phyllis pressed their cocktail shaker into service.

"Ya'll take care if you use them tollets during the night," the lady camped next to us warned. "The wild pigs are like to knock you over runnin' through here in the dark."

Wild pigs? That did not cause much alarm, since we lived around moose and bears, wolves and wolverines. After all, pigs were farm animals, weren't they? We survived the Everglades, past the alligators and panthers. Pigs didn't scare us.

Even so, we thought about wild pigs as we cleaned up after dinner, securing all the food in coolers. As darkness fell, I kept a flashlight near at hand. We lay down to sleep, and I sighed with relief, hearing nothing more than the thrum of night insects. Mom, Phyllis, and Gram stretched out on their aluminum cots, surrounded by thin mosquito net walls.

Over the late evening noises of humming bugs and sleeping kids, Mom stiffened at another sound nearby. Footsteps? A snuffle? As she peered into the darkness, the dim light from the campground shower house reflected in the red eyes of a wild pig staring back at her through the mosquito net.

Her scream brought everyone to attention—in our group, and at several nearby camp spaces.

Hooves trampled.

Fleeing pigs grunted.

Their calls mingled with the metallic crash of Gram's cot as she attempted to disembark, damaging it beyond repair this time. All this, followed by the muttering of tired children, and then the flashlight's glow that enabled Mom and Phyllis to assess the damages.

In stage whispers, they jerry-rigged Gram's bed, at an odd angle and a bit close to the ground, but no more could be done about it until morning.

The next day we packed up, leaving behind the wreckage of the aluminum cot, and headed on toward New Orleans. We shared our "Bay of Pigs" adventure story with others as we headed west.

Even today, campers in any Florida state park might encounter wild hogs. They are found in every county in the state. These are not the wild boars of Europe, but rather a mixture of feral domestic pigs, or hybrids crossing domestic pigs with European wild boars. They are voracious eaters of almost anything and are a regular threat to crops, landscaping, and even some endangered animals such as sea turtles and ground nesting birds.

In September 2016, NPR Radio ran a story about one solution to Florida's half a million problem pigs: prime pork! Keith Mann raised bison and beef cattle on his Three Suns Ranch near Port Charlotte. Mann claimed that this wild pork is 44 percent lower in calories than commercially raised pork. And residents with the means to trap and deliver feral hogs were glad to be rid of them. Unfortunately, Three Suns Ranch has now closed.

Wild hog hunting is popular in Florida, and on private property (with permission, of course) hunting them is almost unrestricted. Hunters are free to bag as many as they want, any time of year, with any weapon that is legal to own. Public lands place more restrictions, but few enough to encourage hunters.

Mom's diary identifies the park as Manatee Springs, a cold-water spring that pours out more than a hundred million gallons a day and provides a haven for manatees. These marine mammals, sometimes called sea cows, can grow to ten or fifteen feet long and usually weigh 1,000 to 1,500 pounds. We enjoyed a brief dip in the pool before it closed, but any interest in manatees was overshadowed by the wild pig invasion.

After a mostly sleepless night for Mom, we drove a few hours to our next camping spot, stopping to replace Gram's bed along the way, and buy some groceries. An ad in the *Lake Charles (Louisiana) American-Press* featured tuna at twenty-five cents a can, ground beef for thirty-nine cents a pound, and Valencia oranges for five cents each. Hamburger buns to go with that ground beef cost nineteen cents for a package of eight. Gram spent about ten bucks to replace her bed.

Like our first night in Florida, we spent our last night at a pre-Civil War fort turned camping area, Fort Pickens on Santa Rosa Island. Mom wrote, *"We saw this huge ship. I think it was an aircraft carrier with guns and everything."*

She was right. Fort Pickens itself was built in the 1830s to defend Pensacola Bay, and across the water lies Pensacola Naval Air Station, a major training center for naval aviators. The carrier Lexington, anchored in the bay, was stationed in Pensacola from 1962 to 1991. The Naval Air Station began as a navy yard built in the early 1800s because live oak trees in the area provided a source of preferred shipbuilding material. In 1914, military leaders chose the site for the development of naval aviation.

Military needs in Vietnam required more pilots, and as we drove through the country in 1965, Pensacola ramped up to meet that need. Pilot training there produced more than 2,500 graduates in 1968, up from about 1,400 in 1962.

Today thirteen Naval Air Stations are active in the United States, and dozens more have been consolidated with other military facilities or decommissioned entirely. Pensacola continues as a primary naval aviation training center and home to the Blue Angels aerobatic flying team.

We would not soon forget Florida's rotten-egg smell, our sunburns, and the wild pigs, but as always, we wanted to see what lay farther down the road. We intended to head to Mexico—all the way to Mexico City—after stops to see friends and family in New Orleans, Texas, and Colorado.

Our route never passed through Arkansas, but we did run into an Arkansas traveler in Mobile, Alabama. I should say, he ran into us.

We navigated a four-lane road, U.S. 90, through city traffic in Mobile, tensions high as we searched the street signs for our next turn in an unfamiliar city. A Cadillac pulled past us in the right-hand lane; we weren't moving fast enough for him. As the driver swung around us and pulled back into our lane, his left rear fender caught on our right front bumper, bending ours forward so the end of it stuck out like a battering ram.

All of us felt the impact, realizing we'd been hit, and chaos erupted in the Wayward Bus. Then he sped away. At least he tried to. He was hemmed in by other cars, now that he occupied the inside lane.

Mom yelled, "Follow him!" to Phyllis as she grabbed a paper and pen. "Mama, read me the license number." We recognized the Arkansas plates, after weeks of searching license plates in our travels, always on the lookout for other Alaskans.

We stayed on his tail and he apparently realized we did not intend to let him escape. He pulled into a Standard gas station.

The attempted hit-and-run counted as a strike against him in our book. When he stopped the Caddie, his passenger, a woman, pushed her door open and swung her feet out onto the hot asphalt of the parking area. Right away, the Arkansas traveler hustled to her side of the car, shaking his head and waving her back inside.

Phyllis and Mom exchanged a glance. Why was he making her stay in the car in that god-awful heat?

"She's probably not his wife," Phyllis whispered.

"Or maybe he doesn't want her around them," Mom said, tilting her head toward the two young black men in service station uniforms.

They chalked up another strike against him. Yes, he was either a racist or a cheating husband.

Mom reported in a letter to Dad the conversation that gave him his third strike:

"When we walked over to him he says with this smart ass smirk, 'Why don't we just call it even. You pay for yours and I'll pay for mine.' Well we naturally didn't go for it so we called the cops and they came right over."

We photographed the damage to our car, and soon the police arrived, two burly but friendly white officers. Our damage matched the scratches on the Cadillac, as well as the version of events Mom and Phyllis described, and the Arkansas traveler received his due citation.

Mom continued: *"We filled out all the proper forms right there and while this one cop was listing the names of the passengers in our car he got to laughing (there wasn't enough space provided on the form) and this all led to a big discussion about Alaska and then they started talking about racial stuff and how the cops in Alabama weren't at all like the TV stories about Selma and they sure didn't want us to think they were like that."*

In the meantime, the men from the service station examined our van with fascination. Alaska license plates with the state flag embossed on them. The camping gear in our roof rack and rear cargo hold. The animal footprint stickers trailing up one side and down the other. They laughed at our motto painted across the back doors of the van: "The hurrier we go the behinder we get."

We told them about our adventures, and soon the police officers joined in friendly banter with the service station men. After the civil rights upheaval we had seen on television, the warnings from Uncle Bill, some of the relations in New York, and occasionally fellow campers about fraternizing with blacks, and the "whites only" signs that persisted on restrooms in the South, their friendliness to one another surprised us.

We get along fine, the cops assured us. Phyllis wrote a letter quoting one as saying the "n———rs" in Mobile had everything they wanted, including equal rights. In his opinion, the communists incited most of the race-related trouble happening. As friendly as it all appeared, his use of that term gave me pause. That was a bad word in our house.

Then their conversation continued something like this: With a grin, one of the cops asked, "You want to see what you see on TV?" He turned with a smile to one of the black guys. "Come on, let's show them how we're 'supposed' to act." He pulled out his billy club and gestured for the young man to lie down on the ground.

In friendly cooperation, they staged a scene of police abuse for our entertainment. The black man on the ground pretended wide-eyed fear while the white police officer, with a foot on his back, pretended to threaten him with his truncheon.

My vast naiveté pains me to recall and to expose it in writing, but that day, I believed what I heard—that the racial strife did not reflect every heart in Alabama. That seemed to be their message, but things are not always as they seem.

At thirteen I was too naïve to consider that the black men cooperated only to avoid certain trouble. That their friendliness may have been as much an act as the scene of abuse they portrayed. Fifty years later, I can see the probability.

Now I recognize that scene as a tragedy rather than an amusement.

The service station attendants bent our bumper back in place, and we asked the police officers the best route to leave the city. One of them offered to escort us. Car 11 of the Mobile Police Department led us to the edge of town and sent us on our way.

The experience fulfilled a prophecy long proclaimed by Uncle Bill, that our Wayward Bus would be run out of town by the cops if we carried out our plans for the Drive. The whole affair slowed us down by a couple of hours.

"It was all quite interesting," Mom wrote of our car accident, *"but I must say enuf excitement for a long time. They had some nice things to say about us and they thought we were good representatives from Alaska."*

As I comb through the letters and stories about this incident, I'm surprised by one omission in all that Mom and Phyllis wrote, describing what happened. They never mention the black men at the service station. In the oral history of the Drive, and in my memory, they were always helpful and curious toward us, and friendly—or at least fully cooperative—with the police. But Mom's letter makes no mention of them, and Phyllis wrote of the incident, too, and said nothing about them.

I can't help but wonder why. They had no reluctance to talk about it, and repeated the story often through the years. But why not commit it to writing? Both Mom and Phyllis wrote their letters the day it happened. Were these racial interactions really so taboo? Were they afraid to talk openly about it until we returned to Alaska, home from our travels in foreign lands like Alabama? How did the attitudes of Uncle Bill and Dad influence what they wrote in their letters home? Bill had definite racial prejudices, and while Dad did not express the same hostility, his approach would certainly have been more guarded than Mom's.

This is one of the questions I'd love to ask but no longer can. When I began writing about the Drive, Phyllis had already died, and her memories of the Drive were erased by Alzheimer's disease, diagnosed in 2007.

Mom lived in a retirement home a few blocks away from me and we often discussed the trip as this writing took shape. She and Phyllis began to write about the Drive soon after our return, imagining the story told entirely through letters—some of those we had actually sent home, and others they created after the fact to fill in gaps and add drama. Because Mom and Phyllis always loved drama.

Mom revived the dream of writing the story of our 1965 adventure, but now I would write it. She encouraged me to keep working on it, always glad to answer my questions, compare memories, and reminisce.

I used Phyllis's stash of letters and paper mementos, frequently referring to the written records and photos she left behind, and my own memories. Mom told me several times that her Drive in '65 records were in a box somewhere, and we searched for them without success. Still, with Mom, Marlie, and Glenn to call on for memories, I hoped the records from Phyllis were enough.

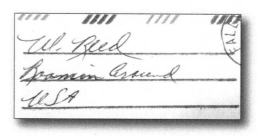

Chapter 15

BETWEEN FLORIDA AND NEW ORLEANS we drove through a fierce rain, with sheets of water sluicing over us. We feared for our gear tied to the top of the van, and for the survival of our wipers, barely able to clear the windshield.

Rain wouldn't be worth mentioning if it weren't so different from rain in Alaska. First is the volume of water. Alaskan rain may fall at a steady, even drenching, rate, but that Gulf Coast downpour flowed over my face so heavily I could barely breathe. Then is the temperature of the rain. In Alaska, rain is cold. Even in the warmth of late summer, rain chills to the bone. But this rain felt as warm as bathwater. I could stand in it soaked to the skin and not feel cold. And the smell—not so much of the rain but the pungent fragrance of moist fertile earth—an aroma so fecund I wouldn't have been surprised to see a magic beanstalk rise from the ground before me and grow a hundred feet into the sky as I watched, like it would in a fairy tale. Our gardens in Alaska didn't smell like that, and nothing grew like magic. Nothing grew without hard work.

What were sharecroppers? We talked about sharecroppers as we passed dilapidated houses lining the country roads, places that looked poor, and the people—some black, some white—looked poor too. The yards held a few old things rusting in the sun. A car, or more useful, a pickup. Maybe a bicycle and a derelict refrigerator. The house paint worn clear off, if there ever had been any, and the people's clothes looked as tired as they did. Mom couldn't explain what it meant to be a sharecropper. She'd never seen one before.

Through the rain, past propped up tin-roofed houses, road-weary cars in yards, skinny dogs barking at the end of their chains, through sharecropper country where the sight of hopelessly poor people on their sagging porches left me wide-eyed and speechless, we aimed toward Slidell, Louisiana, where Aunt Phyllis's close friend Clare lived. We stayed with her family for a couple of nights.

On Saturday July 10, Clare and her husband escorted Mom and Phyllis to the French Quarter, taking in Canal, Basin, and many blocks of Bourbon Street. Mom talked about seeing Al Hirt's place and the great jazz for the rest of her life, especially with her musician friends. She wrote to Dad:

"We walked down Bourbon Street. It was still daylite so we just mosied around looking in the shops. Then we stopped at one place where a Negro was singing up a storm. He was so good, had just a couple of teeth but he could play a mean piano and sing. Songs like "You got the right string baby but the wrong YoYo" and "At the Hogwash Junction Function." He

was a panic. Then we went to the Dixieland Hall and it surpassed anything I could have imagined. I'd have given everything if you could be there. It's in an old old building and no bigger than half our house. You give a donation to get in. A jazz band headed by a guy named Barbarin was playing. They were just fabulous and I could have stayed there all night.

"When we stepped out on Bourbon Street it was dark, but the whole street had come alive with thousands of lights and people. The streets are real narrow with old buildings which all have wrought-iron balconies and some of them have plaques outside saying 'Jefferson Davis ate here' or the names of other historicals engraved. Every other place has a man holding the door open and makin' like a carnival barker. Inside you could see a fantastic display of strippers in every imaginable stage of undress.

"So we just walked down the street gaping like good tourists should and then we came home. I had a rotten headache so I came 'home' and Sandy and I are in bed. It's beautifully quiet and homesicky."

The next day, Phyllis and Mom returned to New Orleans with all the kids, to show us the sights they had so enjoyed. The long, narrow bridge across Lake Pontchartrain, still one of the longest bridges in the world, left my heart pounding as we met trucks barreling toward us with no room to spare. But that offered the best route into the city. Today the bridge, or causeway, includes two spans, but back then it had just one. Driving that two-lane bridge was like being in a tiny boat headed for a distant but invisible shore. Relief flooded me when we reached solid ground more than twenty miles later.

Right away, we headed for Bourbon Street. We strolled past the old buildings, music pouring into the warm air, so humid my clothes stuck to me, but we saw plenty of distractions. Among the crowd of tourists, panhandlers, sailors on shore leave, and jazz fans, people wore colorful costumes—a clown, dance hall girls, men in top hat and tails, sometimes handing out flyers or inviting us to see a show. From the cast-iron balconies above, people-watchers looked down on us, the red tips of their cigarettes glowing in the dusk. Couples walked hip to hip, clinging to one another's waist as they drifted among the music halls, bars, and restaurants. Overwhelmed by the crowds, noise, heat, and aromas of unfamiliar foods, I tried to keep close to our group as I embraced the fascinating scene.

Most of the businesses catered to 'over 21,' but we tried to peer in the doors as we passed. The doormen—part carnival barker and part bouncer— shut the doors when they caught us peeking. Glenn and Jim discovered something useful: if they looked across the narrow street, the doormen of the clubs over there paid no attention to them. The doors remained open, providing a much more complete view of the exotic dancers and inner workings of those adult establishments. Glenn was nine years old, perhaps a little too young to appreciate these attractions, but Jim certainly enjoyed the sights. For a couple of blocks, they saw an eyeful, until Mom and Phyllis caught on to their game and reined them in.

That day, we saw *"What's New Pussycat?"* with Peter Sellers. The movie entertained us all, but a theater with air conditioning attracted us nearly as much as the film.

At eleven in the evening we stopped for dinner, fried shrimp and oysters, with spicy Cajun seasonings that tasted exotic. Long after midnight, we tiptoed back into our sleeping quarters in Slidell and slid into bed with satisfied exhaustion.

Dad's letter of July 5 reached us in Slidell. He enjoyed the Polaroid photos we sent him and sounded a little envious of our experiences. He reported his usual news of the tariff business in Anchorage and freight transfers in Moose Pass but not much more.

Up to this point in the trip, Mom and Phyl's letters home shared our news in positive tones. Though they missed their husbands, their upbeat letters focused on the many sights and new experiences we enjoyed. But by the time we reached New Orleans, we had logged thousands of miles with eight of us packed into the Wayward Bus.

Mom wrote a long letter to Dad at Slidell. After describing our misadventure in Mobile, she says:

"Slidell is quite a town. Lots of poor (sharecropper) Negroes. It's the hottest weather we've had so far, in the high 90s, and so darn humid it's hard to breathe. I'll be so glad to get to Colorado.

After a break in the flow, Mom continued the letter the next day with the comment, *"You can see I get interrupted sometimes. The lack of privacy is killing me. We stayed an extra damn day. Don't ask me why. But we're on our way to Texas. Ever since we got to the coast of Georgia and all around Florida it has smelled swampy. I sure hope it is different in Texas."*

All of us suffered the change of mood depicted in Mom's letter. Hot, homesick, tired of visiting strangers (even those related to us), our good will toward one another wore thin. With the bulk of responsibility on their shoulders, Mom and Phyllis grew snippy with one another. Jim was moody.

Marlie and Mikie played jokes on the rest of us, who failed to see the humor. I found some solace in my occasional turn to ride in the front seat, looking for places of interest and following our route on the map.

I think one of the reasons we stayed "an extra damn day" was to take us kids to New Orleans, because only the adults saw it the first time.

Mom recorded an incident July 12 in her diary. *"This morn as we prepared to leave Slidell I was carrying my satchel across the road and a sheriff hailed me over to ask me all sorts of things. Where are you goin'? Just across the street. Where ya been? Well, I've been staying at a friend's house but we're leaving this morning. Where ya from? Alaska. Is yer Mummy and Daddy with you? My mother is, and that's my 13-year-old daughter over there. Are you sure you're not tellin' me a story, honey? Well, our car's right there with our Alaska plates and I have all kinds of identification here in my purse. At this point he changed his mind and left. Boy I want to get out of the South!"*

Why did he question her this way? Could it be paternalistic overprotection, just a lawman looking out for a young woman alone? Mom clearly felt uncomfortable about this conversation and sensed something beyond public service in the interest he showed. She could laugh off boorish and suggestive behavior among people she knew, but she found this man's questions creepy, whatever his intent.

While Phyllis and Mom visited Bourbon Street, the U.S. Air Force achieved its first air victory in Vietnam, shooting down two MIG-17 fighter jets. The number of U.S. troops in Vietnam rose to 71,000 that week, as the 1st Infantry Division landed at Cam Ranh Bay.

In 2017, Conde Nast Traveler magazine included southern Vietnam as one of seven "Best Places to travel in May" along with such travel headliners as Paris and San Francisco. Photos and books extol the beauty of Vietnam, but my high school and college years were so filled with the troop escalations and death tolls, protests and government coverups, that I still resist envisioning Vietnam as a tourist destination. My visceral negative response fights against my awareness of the lovely land and people today.

Barbra Streisand appeared on the cover of the National Enquirer, Gram's favorite newspaper, with the headline "I was happier as a beatnik." She was discovered in Greenwich Village in 1960 and her career soared in 1964 with the success of Funny Girl on Broadway. In April 1965, at barely twenty-three years old, Streisand hosted her first solo television special, My Name is Barbra, which won five Primetime Emmy Awards. She has won eight Grammy awards and two Oscars and had dozens of nominations in her long career.

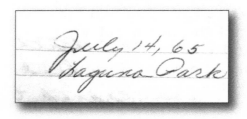

July 14, 65
Laguna Park

Chapter 16

SANDY WAS SO HOMESICK YESTERDAY *she actually cried. Said she was tired of all these strange people,* Mom wrote to Dad on July 12. Marlie suffered bouts of homesickness every so often, and ended one note to Dad with *I miss miss miss miss miss you!* Her homesickness passed quickly, helped by Mikie's readiness to play with her which provided a valuable distraction. I was normally stoic in adversity, which made my tears notable.

The truth is, by July we all struggled with homesickness. New experiences kept our attention, but hours on end in the car no longer counted as a new experience. And the heat exhausted us all. We adapted to cool weather back home by adding a sweatshirt, a coat, or warmer socks, but in hot weather, there's only so much clothing to remove. Even nakedness wouldn't cool us off in the sweltering coastlands or blistering Texas plains.

The long cool twilight evenings of Alaskan summer called to me. Growing up with summer daylight lasting until ten or eleven at night, the sudden sunsets of the South, with blackest night arriving by seven or eight o'clock, left me feeling shortchanged.

Along the Gulf Coast Phyllis pulled in to a weigh station and weighed the Wayward Bus with all of us inside. Five thousand pounds. The vehicle weighed almost three thousand, and Mom estimated eight hundred pounds of people. Our gear, and the never-ending gifts we received along the way—food, tools, clothing, curiosities—contributed to the remaining twelve hundred pounds. Every few thousand miles we sent home a couple of boxes or packages, but it continued to accumulate, and our gas mileage dropped to fourteen miles per gallon with the extra weight.

Speaking of weight, Mom wrote to Dad July 13, *I'm getting a little worried about the kids. Sandy weighs only 88 lbs. (she's taller than me now) and she weighed 94 before we left. Marlie has lost 4 lbs and Glenn lost 1 lb. but they should be gaining cause they're getting taller. I'm sure it's the heat. I've lost 9 lbs but that won't hurt anything.*

Phyl called Bill in Colo. a while ago. He says there's a letter there for me. The kids go wild when they get a letter. I feel so sorry for Sandy. She's been writing dozens of letters, and she hasn't gotten any in return. Mom urged Dad to encourage my cousins and some friends to write to me. I felt sorry for myself, too, which no doubt contributed to my episode of tears.

We stayed a couple of nights at Laguna Park, Texas, in mid-July to visit Sammy and Smiley, a couple who moved there from Moose Pass to enjoy their retirement on the shores of Lake Whitney, north of Waco. They tied up their boat in chest-deep water near the shore to act as a raft. We splashed around to cool off in the hundred-degree heat.

Marlie and Mikie, more comfortable with their dog-paddling skills than I, wanted to learn to dive into the water. Mom patiently coached them, standing near the boat as they clambered up the aluminum ladder and flopped into the water again and again.

"Glenn was standing on the bow watching the whole procedure," Mom wrote. *"Mike and Marlie were total failures at the art of diving. Then out of a clear blue sky Glenn did a beautiful dive. He never said a word, just dove off. (He can't swim, you know.) Then he came up out of the water right where I was standing and grabbed me in a death grip and started crying his head off. He had actually scared the hell out of himself. It was just hysterical. I thought Sammy and Smiley would split. Then it took an act of congress to get him to do it again but he finally did and it really made him the hero of the day. He's always been the underdog in the water because everyone else can swim. But he's the only one of the little ones now that can dive."*

Glenn sent Dad a postcard picturing a barrel of monkeys. His message: *"Dear Dad, I've been having a blast. In tow[sic] weeks I will be in Mexico. I saw a tarantula there big. I learned to dive thee other day. I'm going [to have] lessons at Splashland."*

Mom loved swimming. She grew up swimming in the ponds and at the beaches of Long Island, and swam in lakes and ponds around Seward and Moose Pass in her teens. Maybe she thought that my six weeks of swimming lessons in seventh grade prepared me, but the truth is, I hated all the splashing and dunking that other kids enjoyed so much. My main interest in the water was cooling off.

After our day at the lake, we drove toward

Colorado, too hot for even our flip-flops, piled in a stinky jumble under the back seats. Mom finished her letter that night. *"We made good time today from Laguna Park to Amarillo. Jim will leave on a bus for Kansas at 2:00 a.m. We'll meet Bill in Trinidad, Colorado, tomorrow noon. Had a kinda trying day. Twas so hot and everyone cranky. Phyl doesn't want Jim to go to Kansas but she's letting him go anyway so she's on edge. Some days are like that."*

Jim rode a Greyhound bus to Strong City, Kansas, almost five hundred miles away, to visit his uncle and namesake, Jim Clark, a brother of Phyllis's first husband. I can imagine Phyllis being anxious about letting Jim ride the bus that far on his own, considering his limited experience in the big wide world. Jim desperately wanted to go home but doubted that Bill would allow it, so this gave him a break that might improve his attitude.

Uncle Bill traveled to Colorado for a visit, and we set a particular time to meet him there. Jim happily put off the inevitable conversation with Bill, after his letter confessing to knocking a hole in the wall with his basketball.

Bill met us in Trinidad, as arranged, where we ate lunch at Chuckwagon. *"All you can eat $1.00 adults 60 cents kids."* Then we drove over La Veta Pass, nearly 9,500 feet, and on to Alamosa.

Arriving in Alamosa July 16, we tore into our letters from Dad—one each for Marlie, Glenn, and me, included with a letter to Mom. Dad assured me he'd encouraged my cousins and friends to write me a letter, and enclosed what was no doubt my first rejection letter as a writer, for a story I sent to Reader's Digest. Even then I enjoyed writing and finding curious, unexpected details in research. These impressed my teachers but left my friends and family shaking their heads. Dad also included the grades I'd been haranguing him for in my letters home: four A's and four B's for my seventh-grade efforts.

Marlie's letter included two letters from her pen pal, along with some pictures. Dad encouraged her to write back and ask Mom to take a photo she could enclose. He asked a couple of questions about swimming in the ocean and visiting the zoo. He also mentioned the zoo in his letter to Glenn, and said it was quiet at home with all of us gone.

His letter to Mom began, *"I received your scolding from Port Charlotte."* (Mom had told him in a letter we were all "more than a little disappointed to find no letter from you. We're all feeling a little low and homesick.") *"There is absolutely nothing happening here. I go to Moose Pass every Tuesday night and come home on Friday or Sat. By the time I get the CPT [the business in Moose Pass] bookwork caught up, there is little time left"* for the home business in Anchorage.

Details of business news filled most of the page, along with a few items about the family and some friends. *"Been cookin my own breakfast, doing my dishes in the washer and some of my own clothes. The rest of the housekeeping is going to pot. Will write again to Alamosa if something thrillin happens."*

Uncle Bill's mother, called Moomie, put us up for the week in Alamosa. Phyllis had visited Bill's family and that area before, so she spent much of her time with Bill while his relatives squired the rest of us around the area.

Mom spent a lot of the visit just lying on the floor trying to breathe the thin air at 7,543-feet elevation. She did attend the greyhound races with Bill's sister in her air-conditioned Thunderbird. The loss of twelve dollars didn't diminish the fun of the outing or the excitement she found in gambling.

At one time, dog racing was a major gambling attraction in Colorado. Several tracks opened in the 1940s and '50s, and in 1965 the business was in full swing. After several decades of racetrack success, a state lottery and casino gambling arrived in the 1980s and '90s. Dog racing faded until, by 2008, only one track remained active. Colorado outlawed it in 2010.

When all the other kids swam at Splashland one day, a couple of Bill's relatives took Gram, Mikie, and me out hunting for arrowheads. We drove outside of town to a wide dry valley and spent hours bent over looking at the ground, kicking sand and rocks. Gram and I pointed out plants, rocks, insects, and other finds that impressed us.

I carried a bit of rock to one of our guides, still uncertain of my skills. "Is this something?"

"It sure is. It's the tip of an arrowhead. See the flat edge there? That's where it broke off."

I grinned my thanks and ran to show Gram.

I cherished that broken arrowhead—and another complete one I found. Once in a while I gazed across the barren expanse and wondered who left their arrows here, and what they hunted. We sighted no animals. Could these arrows have been shot at a person?

After a couple of hours we loaded back into the car, Gram and I in the back seat looking over our treasures. A sudden itch and then a sharp pain on my back sent me twisting. Then another on my side.

As I tried to reach that, another burning pain struck my waist. I pulled up my shirt a little and discovered tiny ants crawling on me. Fire ants, with a bite like the stab of a hot pin. The tiny ants crawled so fast I could not remove them, especially in the moving car.

"Take off your shirt," Gram said as she brushed them off.

The pain won out over my embarrassment at needing to undress in front of strangers, and I pulled off my shirt so Gram could swat the ants and kill them. Fortunately they stayed out of my shorts.

At last we conquered the fire ants, and I shook out my shirt and put it back on, greatly relieved to be dressed again before we arrived back in town.

I don't know whether we spent that day on private or public lands, or what the laws of that time and place allowed for gathering arrowheads. Perhaps the adults knew, but I didn't give it a thought. Today, strong restrictions prohibit the taking of any archeological item from federal or Indian lands without a permit, with further regulation of what can be bought, sold, imported, or exported. Native American grave goods and items crafted from endangered or protected species have their own restrictions, regardless whether they are found on public or private lands. In addition, states may enforce further restrictions. Depending on the value of the items involved, such activity could be considered a felony. Our casual afternoon arrowhead hunt should not be repeated today without careful consideration of the legal and ethical issues.

Most of the arrowheads for sale in gift shops today are modern-made, not advertised as artifacts. Caution should be exercised with any labeled as found artifacts, both regarding their authenticity and the legality of selling them.

Back at Moomie's house I showed off my finds. The other kids dismissed my nerdy interest, telling me instead about their trip to the pool, the fun of a long slide into the water, and their improvement at diving. The adults admired my finds, though, and Mom checked out the ant bites whose stings had eased by then. I stashed the arrowheads in my suitcase and sat down to rest, my lower back aching from the hours bent over searching the desert floor.

After their day at Splashland, Marlie and Glenn bore brilliant red sunburns. In my adolescent wisdom, I'd worn a long-sleeved shirt all day to protect myself. Before evening fell, though, I discovered that the sun could burn right through clothing. My back was a slightly calmer shade of red than Marlie's skin, but painful nonetheless. Bunking together on a big sleeper sofa, we woke several times that night to smear more Noxema lotion on each other's backs. In a summer of sunburns, Colorado gave us the worst.

Jim could tolerate all the sun he wanted without burning. His beautiful olive skin simply darkened browner and browner through the summer, possibly the most Italian-looking skin of all my generation's thirty-two first cousins. However, Jim was still visiting his uncle in Kansas, rejoining us shortly before we left Alamosa.

Uncle Bill grew up in Colorado, in small towns and rural areas with quite a few Mexican, Mexican-American, and Native American people. I wasn't aware of his bigotry toward them until I was older. I'm sure he and my mom argued about it, mainly because they argued about almost everything.

Mom's extended family considered raucous argument a form of entertainment. I gradually realized that knowledge and information about the subject under discussion were entirely optional. Many conversations became loud and contentious, and the topic might be anything from hair styles to international politics. Given this environment, my childhood views of Uncle Bill as a person were not tainted by his racial opinions or his concerns about the spread of communism.

Many years later, I visited Phyllis and Bill, by then living in Washington state. He suffered from emphysema and trailed a long oxygen tube around the house. Perhaps he felt nostalgic, sensing his life slipping away, and he began to share with me an event from his teenage years in Colorado. While riding their horses a few miles from town, he and a couple of buddies happened across a Native American girl, a teenager somewhat younger than them, walking along the road.

I sensed his overdue shame as Bill related how he and his friends began to taunt the girl, snapping a whip at her, chasing her if she ran, and terrorizing her. At the time he and his friends considered this great sport, but at eighty years old, he knew they had done wrong and wished he could undo it.

Today's instant communication options make our many letters back and forth seem archaic. In Alamosa, Mom and Dad talked for about ten minutes during a rare phone call that summer. The brief conversation cost Mom fifteen dollars—more than many of our restaurant meals for all eight of us. So, soon after they hung up, Mom wrote another letter to Dad. After asking about the road repairs between Anchorage and Moose Pass, she wrote *"Don't let anybody ever tell you that freeway driving is a nightmare. It's really wonderful. Those fellers that engineer those cloverleafs and exits are geniuses. Any half-wit can stay on the right track. (I can.)"*

About twenty thousand miles of interstate highways threaded across the map in 1965, and our route throughout the summer covered fewer than a thousand miles of them. Those few miles demonstrated the benefits of limited access highways to Mom and Phyl. By 2018 our nation had nearly fifty thousand miles of interstate highways.

Mom received a very welcome letter from Dad before we left Colorado. He gave her additional money and issued a warning not to bring back all of Mexico. The same letter included some less welcome comments about a business he visited. *"They have a new delicious redhead down there who is madly in love with ..... her husband. Damn."* A few of his letters included similar remarks about his attraction to women other than Mom. He also conveyed news and gossip about the failing marriages of various friends, which likely fed her insecurities. Those insecurities probably contributed to growing friction between Mom and Phyllis, too. I'm sure Mom envied Phyllis's long visit with Bill in Colorado.

With a few days in one place, I watched some of the news on television. A new law removed all silver content from future minting of dimes and quarters in America. A dime could buy a pound of tomatoes or carrots or cantaloupe in 1965. And for a quarter, you could purchase a package of instant potatoes or a pound of dates. Put that dime and quarter together, and for thirty-five cents, take home a pound of short ribs. The ten-cent silver coins from 1964 are now worth $1.50 to three dollars, depending on condition. A silver 1964 quarter in average condition sells for $3.50 or more.

During the last days of July, over Vietnam, Soviet-made surface-to-air missiles shot down American fighter planes for the first time.

Bob Dylan's music filled our heads, familiar to us because Mom and Phyllis's three brothers all played guitar and sang the folk and popular music of the day. We belted out "Mr. Tambourine Man" and "It Ain't Me Babe" as we drove the long miles. Dylan, the leading songwriter in American folk music at the time, played an electric guitar at the Newport Folk Festival July 25, ushering in the folk-rock era. His performance generated a storm of opposition at the traditionally acoustic venue. On tour over the next several months, Dylan began playing the first half of his concerts with acoustic guitar and the second half with electric. Today, the "Electric Dylan controversy" is covered in full detail on its own Wikipedia.com page.

Chapter 17

On July 26 we cruised south across New Mexico, bent on seeing Carlsbad Caverns. New Mexico surprised me. It was not the flat square of tan desert that I imagined when I studied a map but rather green and hilly in the north with the colorful southern desert studded with buttes and rock tower formations. A red snake slithered across the highway in front of us, and the quantity and variety of cactus plants impressed me.

As we approached Roswell, the van slowed. I looked up, determined not to miss anything worth slowing down for.

"Oh, no!" Phyllis moaned, pulling to the side of the road. "The bloody thing is overheating."

The barren landscape around us shimmered with the afternoon heat. Phyllis shut off the engine.

"So now what?" Jim groused.

"Now we let it cool for a while."

"Oh, geez!" Jim turned away in disgust. "How long is that gonna take?"

From the back seat, Mom said, "Let's just pass around a couple of pops from the cooler, and see how it's doing in a few minutes."

Our Wayward Bus quickly switched into a solar oven. Even with cool drinks, and fanning ourselves with hats or anything handy, the stifling air offered no hint of breeze.

Ten or fifteen minutes later, Phyllis cranked the engine again, and we eased onto the road. In Roswell she pulled into a Texaco station. The local accents were still new to us, but we understood well enough when the attendant said he "deed not know what eet could be."

Mom wrote home to Dad about the rest of our day:

"We drove on to Carlsbad (78 miles south) and by this time it was dark so we got a spot at a private campground run by this bearded Pecos Bill type. After we got the damn bus unloaded we noticed this god-awful odor. It was impossible to tell where it was coming from, but we were sure something had died close by. But we had been in campgrounds that smelled many times—in Florida especially, so we decided to stick it out."

Mom, Phyllis, and Gram, sleeping next to the van under the roll-out tent, experienced the worst of the odor. Gram opened her bottle of Tweed perfume and dampened a Kleenex, which she held by her nose all night, sweetening but not eliminating the odor of raw sewage. Mom detested Tweed perfume ever after. Jim and I, sleeping at the back of the van and farthest from the stench, escaped the worst, but none of us slept well.

"No one has ever had such fantastic luck as this crew. We were within inches of a double sewer vent— we discovered this in the morning after we spent half the night burning incense which I'd bought (29 cents)

for Helen Nagy. We broke camp at 6 a.m. (the kids were even willing), drove back to the city of Carlsbad to have the car looked at, at a Chevy garage. They tightened the fan belt. He said he'd never heard of a Corvair engine overheating. He also checked the wiring (the blinkers are on the blink—ho ho). All this while we were led to a coffee room to wait—a lovely place—the bill? $1.55.

"One hour out of Carlsbad on the way to the caverns the darn light came on saying the engine was hot. We've finally decided that it's a combination of the heat and the high altitude. We had no trouble between the caverns and El Paso. It's either flat or downhill, but it's the most desolate stretch of ground we've hit so far. There are only two or three gas stations in that 140 miles (Highway 62-180) and there's not another living thing (that we could see, thank God)."

We camped over the sewer vent near White's City, New Mexico. Businessman Charlie White bought acreage near the entrance to Carlsbad Caverns National Park in the early 1900s and developed his tourist trap. Motels, campgrounds, and restaurants are supplemented by entertainment and specialty shops. Through three succeeding generations of the family, White's City added businesses, gained a U.S. Post Office, and thrived.

Exploring the town, we couldn't resist a visit to the Million Dollar Museum. Mom's letter described it: *"Had human skeletons thousands of years old (even one from a cliff dweller) for Sandy to see, and the most fantastic doll house collection. Two or three rooms of them over 100-200 years old, from many foreign countries—Germany, Holland, etc. Mostly European. All very detailed, including not only the furniture but dishes, curtains, even toothpicks. Marlie and Mikie were in their glory. Glenn enjoyed the old cars, horse-drawn hearse, branding irons, ancient looking typewriters and sewing machines."*

Carnival booths and a curved mirror entertained us all, along with the baby alien, the collection of old typewriters, and a room filled with cow horns. We didn't own a flash camera, but those who want to see pictures can find them on the internet.

On July 14, 2008, Charlie White's heirs sold the entire city and all its assets at auction. The *Albuquerque Journal* reported that the 366-acre town, including significant water rights, sold for $1.55 million.

The contents of the Million Dollar Museum sold at auction separately, and the museum closed. Reading about it, I wondered who bought the mummies. Then I found an article saying that the FBI collected all the human remains prior to the sale, for DNA testing.

The real reason people drive to the desolate southeast corner of New Mexico is not White's City but the stunning cave system known as Carlsbad Caverns. The caverns awed us, as they do hundreds of thousands of visitors every year. The largest chamber, the Hall of Giants, encompasses a floor space of more than eight acres. I could only imagine all the unexplored branches of caves, completely invisible from the desert above, and I wondered about the people who first explored them, perhaps sheltered in them at times, or maybe even died there. Yes, my imagination raced through the rough passages, dodged dripping stalactites and towering stalagmites. My imagination explored the outer reaches—but not me. The adventure of seeing the Hall of Giants, within sight of the park rangers, was enough.

Though the temperatures aboveground were scorching hot, underground the temperature held steady at fifty-six degrees, cool enough that I rubbed my bare arms, wishing for a sweater.

Eerie shadows filled the corners behind towers of layered sediment and fingers of stone stretching down from the ceiling. After listening to the ranger's talk, we left the cavern in elevators, installed in 1932 so more people could visit, because the trek uphill to leave the caves proved too difficult for many.

We were among the 591,000 people who visited the park in 1965. Recreational visits peaked in 1976 at more than 875,000. During the past ten years, only about 400,000 people per year visited Carlsbad Caverns. In 2018, the number of visitors topped 500,000 for the first time this century.

The park includes 119 caves but only three are open to the public. Because of the sensitive cave structures and ecosystems, most are limited to entry by scientific researchers. Since we visited in 1965, further exploration revealed several additional caves, as recently as 2013. No doubt more secrets of the cavern system remain for future explorers to discover.

We spent that night at La Fonda Motel in El Paso before heading into Mexico. On ebay.com I found vintage postcards picturing the motel. Its low-profile Spanish-style facade with a series of arches along the front and tile roofs—very typical architecture for the area—looked exotic to Alaskan kids. Mom does not mention the cost of the rooms, but if other costs recorded for the trip are any indicator, I would probably spend more to buy three old postcards than we paid to stay there in 1965.

We played and swam in the hotel pool until ten-thirty at night and slept soundly until Mom and Phyllis woke us.

"Get up! Get up!" they called. "Today we're going to Mexico!"

That day, July 28, Juarez (the city across the border from El Paso) hosted meetings with American consular officials about plans to speed up border crossings for Mexicans entering the U.S. We were headed the other direction, but Mom needed 16-millimeter movie film, and we spent a couple of hours looking for a store that sold it. With film in hand, we headed for the border and used another hour obtaining tourist passes, insurance, and Mexican money.

Finally, we crossed the Rio Grande.

Chapter 18

THOUGH WE HAD ALREADY EXPERIENCED many strange and new places—New England and Long Island, Washington, D.C., and the Deep South, the wide plains and cowboy country—I knew now we truly headed into foreign lands.

We aimed for Mexico City. Phyllis wrote to Bill, describing our entrance:

"We didn't have any trouble at the border. They opened up the back doors and decided it wasn't worth it and stamped it all OK and we got our permits, etc. When we were allowed on we crossed a bridge onto a little street in Juarez and found to my horror that I didn't know where to go. So as usual made the wrong decision and made a left on a one-way street going right. Several men yelled and I then made a U turn at the intersection and was going to go right when someone else yelled, 'This way.' So I backed up again and headed 'that way.' A real nice looking Mexican told me which way to go to find Mexico City. We didn't find the highway the way he said so finally had to ask

again. The first one couldn't speak English so wouldn't even answer, just shook his head no. Finally found someone to tell us we were two blocks from the right street so we headed down the highway."

With all that behind us, we thought our troubles over. We forged ahead, across miles and miles of Mexican desert country, populated by cactus, tarantulas, and the occasional skinny cow. The landscape differed little from New Mexico, but the buildings and the clothing and the language put us solidly south of the border. I sensed the "otherness" of a foreign land. Tangible differences like road signs in Spanish and houses of adobe added to the intangible, atmospheric differences. I knew if we broke down and needed help, we might not find someone who spoke English to help us.

Though I knew Canada was a different country, the language and culture were more familiar. Mexico wasn't simply a foreign country, but in Mexico I was a foreigner, something I never felt so keenly before. I sensed it more and more as I tracked our progress on the map in my lap, inching our way toward Mexico City.

I spotted something along the roadside ahead. "Gram, what's that?"

As we drew near, she inhaled sharply. A dead cow, just off the road's shoulder.

"Do you think it just starved to death?" I couldn't imagine why someone hadn't fed it better, but the ribs showed on most of the cows we saw.

Gram thought a minute. "Maybe a car hit it. Like the moose sometimes get hit back home."

We noticed no injuries as we drove by. Before the day ended, we passed the carcasses of two more cows, lying in the ditch near the ubiquitous prickly pears.

Coming toward us along one stretch was a truck

loaded with large sticks or branches—and I mean loaded, hanging over each side of the flatbed by at least three feet and rising above the truck's cab, tied down with ropes. We edged to the shoulder of the road to pass.

The adobe buildings in the towns we drove through drew my gaze, as did the old church buildings with twin bell towers rising over the rooftops, and the colorful woven and embroidered clothing. I watched a man holding a plow steady as his horse pulled it across a dry field, raising dust that trailed off to one side in the breeze.

A big argument between Mom and Phyllis along an isolated stretch of road a few hours south of the border shattered the charm of Mexico. Snide comments back and forth, and glares I could see from the back seat, erupted in yelling. Phyllis pulled to the side of the road, and the argument continued.

Everything inside me screamed "Stop!" My heart thumped, nerves jangling as I considered that this could end the trip and erect a wall between our family and Phyllis's. I wanted to do something to calm things down, but what?

"Mom, Phyllis, come on..." I began, my voice shaking. I reminded them of all our effort and planning to make this adventure happen. "It's not just you guys. We worked hard for this too."

Marlie and Mikie chimed in their agreement, and Glenn pressed his back to the seat, tense and wide-eyed. Phyllis and Mom continued sniping.

Jimmy shoved his way to the side doors, jumped out of the van, and stomped off back toward Texas.

"Jim, you come back here!" Phyllis yelled. Then she reversed the van closer to him. "Come on, Jim."

"Not if you guys are screaming at each other." He kept walking.

Phyllis and Mom exchanged a glance. "Okay, we're done. Get back in now. You can't walk home from Mexico!"

Mom scrambled from the van and strode toward Jim. "Come back, Jim. The argument is over."

Jim hesitated, then swiveled, shoulders slumped, and returned to the van. We rode in the silence that follows a storm. The Wayward Bus seemed more wayward than ever as we looked for a place to spend the night.

Phyllis said this about the argument, in her letter to Bill:

"Had a big argument in the car tonight & hope it has cleared the air, at any rate we are headed south in the morning. I have such a bad case of homesickness I can hardly stand it—if I didn't have our car with us I'd catch a bus back to Alamosa and hitch hike home if necessary."

Most of the angry arguments I witnessed at home involved Mom's late nights of play rehearsal or Dad's drinking, problems I thought I understood. But Mom and Phyllis carried on their argument with innuendo that eluded me. Longing for home certainly raised the tensions for both of them. No doubt Mom envied the conjugal visit Phyllis enjoyed during our week in Colorado, and the fact that Bill cared enough to join us there for a week. But some further undercurrent hid in veiled language I couldn't decipher, and which they didn't intend for the kids to understand—grown-up secrets of some kind, and I wasn't grown up yet. Some issues I did understand, though, and Mom's diary records: *"Sandy was quite active in our discussion earlier and spoke her piece with an amazing amount of insight and intelligence."*

Heck, I just wanted to finish the trip.

In any event, our carload of bristling porcupines smoothed its quills and continued south. Phyllis and Mom airing grievances, and Jim's attempted escape, defused the explosive atmosphere, and we carried on to Chihuahua where we checked into two large air-conditioned rooms, with tiled floors, for twelve dollars.

"Or rather 150 pesos" Phyllis reported to Bill.

About the money, she said: *"I traded $105.00 American at the bank at the border and got back 1,311.45. Sure looks like a lot of money, also found another horrible fact—they don't take credit cards here for gas so we'll be paying cash for our gas."* An essential element of our financial planning required all our fuel bills to be paid by Dad and Uncle Bill, as we charged all gas to a credit card, and used our cash for other expenses. Now almost ten weeks into the trip, cash reserves dwindled.

I loved my first-year Spanish class in seventh grade, and Phyllis studied Spanish at the community college since moving to Anchorage. Despite our efforts, we soon recognized the significant limitations of our language abilities. With patience, hand gestures, and a Spanish-English dictionary, we communicated adequately. The younger kids looked to us for translations and explanations and couldn't understand why we were so flummoxed when anyone spoke to us.

We spent a night in Torreon, a long day's drive south of Chihuahua, and mailed letters home from Fresnillo, farther south. Many more miles lay ahead before we arrived in Mexico City.

Mom wrote: *"Mexico so far has been hot, dry, gay, frightening, funny, friendly, hostile, and wonderfully foreign and different. To tell you the truth I've seen enough of it but we haven't spent any pesos yet and* *we must do that of course! We are in Torreon at the junction of Highway 49 and 40, staying at the only motel for miles around. Tho this is a big city. Last night we stayed in a motel in Chihuahua that was absolutely beautiful. Brightly colored tile indoors and out, huge swimming pool. Marlie promptly got acquainted with a slightly inebriated Mexican chap at the pool who thought she was a lovely child. No sooner had I gone out and rescued her (after Mikie squealed) than she struck up a conversation with a German lady in the next room who has a daughter in Point Barrow. The German lady was very nice tho, and we had a long talk. We had two rooms in Chihuahua—adjoining, with baths and kitchenettes for 150 pesos or $12.00 total. This place is more expensive. Three rooms with bath no kitchen (6 beds) for 190 pesos total. Tonight we had dinner a la grande for $11.00. It's such fun.*

"*South of Chihuahua things get green and mountainous. Lots of corn fields, goats, cattle, and horses. Have to be very careful of the cows on the highway. Most of the countryside looks primitive, mud houses, no cars.*"

The families, usually traveling on foot along those highways, did not appear to me as hopelessly poor as the black families in their roadside shacks in Georgia. These people headed somewhere with a sense of purpose. There must have been more small towns than we could see from the road. Otherwise, where could they have been traveling with baskets on their heads or in a homemade cart pulled by a donkey?

All the way south, Gram kept waiting for the town of Despacio. We passed many signs, but we never reached the town. Eventually, when Phyllis realized Gram expected to see a town by that name, she enjoyed a hearty laugh and explained that "despacio" meant slow.

The acres of prickly pear cactus we passed also fascinated Gram. She'd heard they were edible and wanted to taste one. We stopped by the roadside while Mom picked a few, and she and Gram spent the next hour and a half with a pair of tweezers picking the nearly invisible stickers from her hands. I'm not sure we ever did try to eat them.

Mom wrote in her diary, *"The land keeps getting greener, cooler, and prettier as we go south."* Counter-intuitive as that was to us—shouldn't the temperature be hotter as we drove south?—the elevation rose and we all appreciated a break from the heat.

The evening of July 30 we reached San Luis Potosi, more modern than anything we had seen so far in Mexico. Phyllis and I had been sure our knowledge of Spanish would smooth the way for us all. Confident in her abilities, Phyllis walked into a clothing shop with Mom for a closer look at embroidered dresses they'd seen in the window. The sales lady offered to help them.

"No, thank you. We're just looking," Phyllis attempted to say, in her best first-year Spanish.

The clerk frowned and looked from Phyllis to Mom and back, then hurried away.

Mom and Phyllis exchanged a glance, and then a light dawned in Phyl's face. She burst out laughing and grabbed Mom's arm, heading for the door.

"What's the matter?" Mom demanded. "What did you say to her?"

Phyllis was laughing too hard to answer. Down the sidewalk a distance, Mom continued to harangue her. Finally, she choked out, "I thought I said we were just looking, but I said 'No thanks, we're just kissing.'"

They enjoyed a big laugh together. Then Phyllis said, "Come on, let's go back and look at those dresses."

Mom wanted nothing to do with it. She wasn't about to show her face to the clerk again.

As we drove through Mexico, President Johnson announced the commitment of an additional fifty thousand American troops to the conflict in Vietnam. Consequently, the draft would increase to about a thousand young men each day. The first four thousand American paratroopers arrived in Vietnam as we drove between Chihuahua and Torreón.

President Johnson also established Medicare and Medicaid when he signed the Social Security Act of 1965. The *Amarillo (Texas) Globe-Times* ran a series of articles explaining the benefits offered, repeatedly identifying Medicare as a 'government welfare' program. While Medicare would cover hospital services, it would not cover the fees of physicians and specialists. Those expenses would be covered by government-backed insurance, according to the article, which a person over age sixty-five could buy for three dollars per month.

Back in Alaska, the Alaska Purchase Centennial Commission planned the centennial celebration of Alaska's purchase from Russia in 1867, a deal which Secretary of State William Seward negotiated for about two cents an acre. Many mocked the acquisition, calling it "Seward's Folly." By 1965, Alaska had long since proved a worthwhile purchase, with an enormous fishing industry, oil and gas resources, and significant military defense locations.

MARSELLA 28
MEXICO 6, D. F.

Chapter 19

I GRIPPED THE WINDOW HANDLE, white-knuckled, as we drove through Mexico City. The traffic traumatized me. There was just so much of it! Could this be why, when I turned sixteen, I didn't want to learn to drive?

Mom wrote: *"On Saturday evening we pulled into Mexico City. We had a map and an address for a motel. Phyl was driving and first thing we did was go the wrong way down a one-way street (4 lanes wide— My God!) It really wasn't Phyl's fault cause none of us could read the signs. Anyway a cop saw us and waved us over to stop. He was very disgusted and hollered in Spanish but soon realized we hadn't the foggiest notion as to what he was saying so he led us to an intersection and stopped 16 lanes of traffic so we could be on our way."*

We arrived at the motel Phyllis hoped to stay in, but they had no vacancies. After forty phone calls, Mom claimed in her letter, we found two rooms at

Hotel Meurice, available for only one night. Mom continues:

"One of the fellows from the motel escorted us to the hotel then offered us his services for the next day in touring the city (at a reduced price of course from the regularly advertised prices). He spoke very good English and looked honest. He also had all kinds of official-looking credentials (like the F.B.I.) so we gave him a $50 deposit and he left."

He agreed to send a driver to guide us to all the places we wanted to see—the marketplace, the Ballet Folklorico, the famous floating gardens of Xochimilco, and a bullfight!

By this time, Mom and Phyllis knew better than to rely on our own driving and language abilities. We needed a guide in Mexico City. Their chance encounter with the man at the motel was a great stroke of luck, Mom and Phyllis assured us. Only later, as we sat in the restaurant at dinner, did it occur to them that they did not write down the name of the driver who would pick us up or his phone number. How would they even know him if he did show up? And the man from the motel had the fifty bucks.

Dad and Bill worried about just this kind of naiveté, which, for the most part, we managed to avoid during our first fifteen thousand miles on the road. A sick sensation overwhelmed them both as they realized their foolishness—not quite as sick as the feeling that later came over Phyllis and Jim.

"Arrived Mexico City July 30." Phyllis wrote this letter to Bill. *"Finally found a hotel, this being the busy season. Anyway they told us we could have this room for one night only, so we got settled and went down to eat. I got feeling worse and worse and finally*

came upstairs without touching my $2.00 T-bone steak, and got sicker than a dog. Jimmy came up with me and helped me out of the bathroom. They finally called a doctor (what a character he is) and he said it was typical food poisoning. Ordered Chloromycetin, Levadura, and Epsom salts. So then later that evening Jimmy got sick. This morning the doctor came again and said I was much better & Jimmy was even worse than I had been, so he's dosed up too. He wouldn't let us go out so he went down and told Hotel Mgr. that we had to stay no matter what. So they called me and said I made a lot of trouble but we could stay one more night but please get out tomorrow.

"Today the rest went to do all the things they should do and we decided we'd head north in the morning and the heck with it. We'll be leaving tomorrow and will be back in El Paso in 4 or 5 days.

"Since I missed everything, you're going to have to bring me to Mexico again—only we fly to Mexico City and go on a tour."

In spite of the night disrupted by gastrointestinal distress, those of us who weren't sick still wanted to see the city. Mom and Gram, along with Glenn, Mikie, Marlie, and I, headed out to meet our guide.

We stood on the sidewalk, in awe of the wild traffic speeding by, the sounds of a strange language in our ears. Mom fretted about the fellow they hired, wondering if we'd ever see him or the money again. Suddenly a handsome young man approached us, and Mom became flustered, struggling to remember the name they failed to write down.

"Are you Lolita?" she asked.

"Lolita!" He burst out laughing. "I Lalito!"

We joined the laughter and began to relax after the tension of waiting and wondering. The man Mom and Phyllis paid, who spoke English so well, had sent Lalito as our driver. He didn't speak English at all. However, he knew the city well, which provided a big advantage over driving anywhere on our own.

I wrote to Dad: *"I had lots of fun in Mexico. We took a tour around the city with a guy who couldn't speak English. We had lots of fun trying to talk to each other. We saw drunks and beggars and peddlers all around. The people don't drive carefully at all.*

"First we went to the Mexican ballet. There were 9 parts and only 2 or 3 I didn't like." I described dances about the women's role in the revolution, the sugar harvest, a fiesta in Veracruz. *"All the ladies wore white dresses trimmed with red. The slips had red bows around the bottom. A man and lady tied a bow with their feet."* My favorite was a Christmas celebration with *"a big piñata like a satellite."*

The ballet presented dances from many periods of Mexico's history, the first professional ballet any of us, even Mom and Gram, ever saw. We enjoyed the spectacle on stage, and the building that housed it presented a spectacle of its own.

The Palacio de Bellas Artes, or Palace of Fine Arts, replaced an older National Theater of Mexico. Completed in 1934, the columns and arches of the white Carrara marble façade, topped by a dome topped by a winged statue, left a bold impression. But the interior, with its soaring ceiling, murals along rows of proscenium arches, and private boxes, each with a separate balcony front, layered up the side walls, proved stunning. Best of all was the glass curtain, a creation of Tiffany's in New York, comprised of nearly a million pieces of iridescent glass. The pattern depicts two of Mexico's volcanos. The foldable glass creation, the only one of its kind in the world, weighs about twenty-four tons.

Alaska's theatrical venues could hardly compare. Mom had acted in several plays with Anchorage Community Theater, most of them performed in a large Quonset hut building on Minnesota Drive, back when Minnesota was one long mudhole of a road through Spenard. Today it is called the Walter J. Hickel Parkway, a major thoroughfare, and Anchorage boasts sophisticated performance venues. Back then, Alaska Methodist University owned an intimate theater in the round, and the military bases had multipurpose rooms with stages. The Fourth Avenue Theater downtown showed movies, not live productions.

We watched the ballet from high in the cheap seats, in awe of our surroundings as much as the dances. Two copies of the program survive among the Drive in '65 memorabilia, describing the dances in the Ballet Folklorico. Tiny figures on the stage far below played out those scenes from Mexico's history.

My letter goes on: "*Thieves market was real crazy. There was old things and new things. One table was full of doctor things. Mom and I got shoes there.*" But that's not what I remember most—something happened that I didn't mention to Dad or anyone else.

The outdoor market offered welcome space between us, after spending three long days in the van. I wandered, allowing myself a few yards of separation from the others as I peered into stalls shaded by canvas tarps propped on poles, where chattering vendors sold baskets, snacks, and souvenirs. When someone pushed right up against me in the crowded market, I spun around to look. There, directly behind me, a man rushed away and disappeared into the crowd. I realized, with disgust, that he had been pressing against my back, and enjoying it way too much. That ended my market wandering, and I stayed close to Mom, Phyllis, and Lalito as we shopped for souvenirs—a sombrero, wooden toys, and woven handbags. Marlie and Mikie purchased tiny leather sandals for their Barbie dolls. We bought marionettes of sticks, leather, and cheap fabric, which occupied our time in the van as we tried to make them dance and perform plays.

I remembered reading about Xochimilco's floating gardens, near Mexico City, and couldn't wait to see them at our next stop. But the gardens didn't float anymore, which was quite a disappointment. Masses of flowers, and the decorated boats carrying us and other visitors, created a colorful spectacle. I wrote to Dad: *"We ate lunch on a gondola called Rosamaria. There are 2,300 boats on the lake. They were all out when we got there and we kept bumping into them. There were people on the other boats selling flowers, jackets, and dolls."*

At one time a large lake and a canal system separated Xochimilco as its own city. A thousand years ago, farmers built wooden rafts from juniper trees and put soil and mud from the lake bed on them to create additional garden space. These *chinampas* would sink and be replaced by a new raft, eventually creating square islands in the lake. The canals provided a water-borne crop delivery system to many communities.

Mexico City's sprawl engulfed the area, farmers created more artificial islands, and people drained the lakes to accommodate the growing population.

Unauthorized homes built on artificial islands damaged water quality and the environment. The colorful *trajinera* boats still ply the remaining canal. Though Xochimilco was named a World Heritage Site in the 1980s, efforts to save the "floating gardens" proved unsuccessful. In 1965, more than six million people lived in Mexico City's metropolitan area. Today the population exceeds twenty million.

We drifted among the bright floral displays on our hired *trajinera* and enjoyed the mariachi music from live bands on other boats. My disappointment faded amidst the color and music, the sunshine and crowds of other people enjoying the same relaxing ride around the lake.

Next, Lalito drove us to another classic Mexican experience of the time—a bullfight. I watched with morbid fascination as the picadors stabbed their "picks" into the bull, which bled from wounds festooned with the colorful barbs, and reported to Dad that *"I was almost the only one who liked the bullfight."*

"The bull in the first fight jumped the fence. When he got back in he threw a guy on his horns. That bull died best. He died as soon as he was stabbed. One of the picadors on horses got thrown on the ground and almost trampled. Another matador tripped and he got horned a little but not bad."

Not bad? What was I thinking??

An eighteen-year-old bullfighter entered the ring for his first fight. After taunting the bull with his cape and deft movements a few times, the bull gored and severely injured him. Others distracted the bull while picadors carried the young man from the ring. After a few minutes he returned, to the raucous cheering of the crowd, with a bloodied bandage wrapped around his waist and hips. Again he addressed the bull and killed it, to the delight of the bullfighting fans.

Lalito picked us up at the appointed time, and as we loaded into the car, he told us the young bullfighter died of his injuries. The whole affair horrified Mom; if Phyllis had been well enough to attend, Mom may have skipped it. The experience gave us a lot to think about in regards to animal cruelty and foolish risk-taking.

What inured me to the violence and cruelty of the experience? As a child I watched my parents butcher mountain goats and sheep to fill the freezer with food. I had whacked a fish on the head after reeling it in. But bullfighting drapes tradition and pageantry over the killing of an animal, though today most bulls killed in bullfights are processed for human consumption. I would not want to see it now.

Mexico City has the largest bullfighting ring in the world, the Plaza de Toros, completed in 1946 and seating 48,000 people. Bullfighting remains popular in several Latin American countries as well as Spain, France, and Portugal.

Although controversial today, in some countries bullfighting has been proclaimed part of the nation's, or region's, cultural patrimony, bolstering its status and legitimacy. Since 2013, three Mexican states banned bullfighting, and other countries enacted successful limitations on bullfighting as well.

News of the bullfighter's death subdued us as Lalito drove to the hotel. We were sorry to say goodbye to Lalito, perhaps Marlie more than the rest. She had quite a crush on our handsome driver.

Phyllis and Jim recovered enough to travel, and the next morning we headed north—now well and truly homeward bound, although home was still several thousand miles away. None of us felt very well, and that, combined with our exhaustion from the frantic day of touring Mexico City, left us a very crabby carload.

With the songs from *Mary Poppins* still on our minds, we spent time in the car writing new words to the tune of Supercalifragilisticexpialidocious.

We heard about old Mexico and there we had to go
But our story doesn't end right there,
there's more that you should know.
We saw the sights of Mexico, the beautiful ballet,
And the matador at the bullfight
where the people shout Ole!

We dined on enchiladas and swam in waters blue.
We ate the most exotic food
and drank the brewiest brew.
We paid for everything we did.
We paid, oh heaven knows!
We'll sum it up in one more verse,
and this is how it goes:

We went down to Mexico all feeling very merry,
Checked into a nice hotel, just for temporary,
Then we discovered all of us had got the dysentery.
We're goin' back to the USA
where the food is sanitary.

That's how we felt about it as we drove away from Mexico City at the beginning of August in 1965. Now, with a better understanding of intestinal flora, we wouldn't call the food unsanitary, and we might prepare ourselves better for international dining. Bottled water wasn't readily available then, and we didn't know what foods were likely to cause digestive issues. We were living and learning—the very reason we made the Drive.

Chapter 20

HEADING NORTH FROM MEXICO CITY, we planned to drive the most direct route back to El Paso, then visit the Grand Canyon on our way to California and Disneyland.

Mom wrote to Dad: *"The kids don't even care about seeing Disneyland as much as they want to go home, so we might be making new plans when we get to the border. Glenn's birthday today. I bought him a Mexican cake for 15 pesos."* We kids had been as excited about visiting the Magic Kingdom as anywhere along the way. Now, our road weariness began to show.

We drove as far as San Luis Potosi that day, through Mexican countryside that now looked more familiar and friendly, even though we'd been in Mexico less than a week. At the Motel Tuna that night, we played in the kidney-shaped pool. In the morning we pointed the car north again. Here's a letter Mom wrote that night:

"As you can see by the postmark, we are now in Monterey. If you have been following our route on the map, it may seem that we are going in the wrong direction. We are! We took the wrong road out of San Luis Potosi this morn and didn't discover it for 2 hours so we will be crossing the border at Laredo, then go up (northwest) through Carlsbad again and thence to the Grand Canyon. And I'm sure we'll never hear the end of it."

We did drive north out of San Luis Potosi but mistakenly veered northeast rather than northwest. Phyllis added this in a letter to Bill from Monterey:

"We are in the middle of an electrical storm and the electricity is off. Everyone is out on the porch with our radio going enjoying the cool rain etc and I guess the rest of the people in the place think we are crazy. I am writing this with the light of our lantern (battery) so I guess that will be all for today anyway."

With each flash of lightning, the wet foliage and colored tile lit up around us, a startling display of light and thunder. Lightning storms rarely occurred in southcentral Alaska. I'd seen them earlier that summer, but never before.

Inside one of our motel rooms, Phyllis and Mom prepared our cold supper by lantern in the kitchenette, with the power out. They paid no attention as I slipped in.

I quietly eased to the floor by one of the beds and pulled two socks from a nearby suitcase. Then I slid under the bed. They chatted together in the semi-darkness making sandwiches.

I fired a balled-up sock across the floor.

Phyllis screamed. "What was that?" She danced around in the dim light, looking around the room.

"What?"

"I think there is a mouse in here!" Phyllis peered under the table in the semi-darkness.

"Really? It's a clean place."

"Well some bloody thing ran across my foot."

I launched another sock, this time hitting Mom, who jumped with a squeal.

"There it is again! I told you something is in here." Now both of them looked at the floor tiles and dark corners.

I was out of ammo and struggled to keep from laughing out loud at their frantic search for the supposed mouse.

Phyllis stomped across the room. "I'm not staying in this room with a bloody mouse." She grabbed a broom from the corner and jabbed it under the edges of the counter and then along the walls. "Bring the light over here."

Unable to see the socks in the dim light on the patterned tile floor, Mom lifted the lantern and Phyllis poked under the furniture, closer and closer to my hiding place.

I was busted. I slid out from under the far side of the bed, bursting into laughter.

"Stop! There's no mouse. It was me." I retrieved the socks and held them up to the lantern light.

They were not amused.

"Get over here and help with these sandwiches, if you don't have anything better to do than cause trouble," Mom grumbled.

I grinned silently in the dim light as I set napkins and cans of soda on the table. "Anything else?" I glanced over to see Mom and Phyllis trying to stifle their laughter.

"Come here, you little turkey," Phyllis said, grabbing me in a hug. "Go call the rest of them in to eat."

On August 5 we reached the U.S. border. After glancing at our loaded roof rack and peering into the packed rear cargo space, the customs officer asked how long we stayed in Mexico.

"About a week," Mom said.

"Did you buy anything that you are bringing back into the U.S.?"

"Yes, we all bought souvenirs."

He wanted the details.

"Kids, bring out the stuff you bought in Mexico to show the man." Mom retrieved her own woven straw hat from the front floorboards. Jim laid his sombrero on the table, while Marlie and Mikie pulled out their satchels and pawed through the clothes, setting out Barbie doll sandals and sweaters they bought at the market. Glenn added a pair of marionettes he'd been learning to operate.

Phyllis found an embroidered dress in the laundry box, and then said, "Oh, I bought this too!" She shook a tambourine lightly, then set it with the other items, piling up fast.

By this time, all the van doors stood open. The customs agent looked in the back and under the seats. He stood and faced Mom and Phyllis. "Are you bringing in any alcohol?"

They showed him a bottle of tequila.

"What's in that bottle under the seat?"

The exchanged a startled glance and bent to see.

"Ooooh, that," Phyllis said, reaching for a gallon wine bottle stoppered with a cork. "That's vinegar. We had it when we went into Mexico last week."

He looked skeptical, so Mom hurried to explain.

"When we visited our uncle in Florida, he had this

homemade wine, but it turned to vinegar, so he kept what he needed and gave the rest to us. For making salad dressing."

"Vinegar?" Pursing his lips, he waved the car behind us into the next lane. "Okay, unload the rest of your things here." He indicated a row of tables next to the car, one of which already held our Mexican souvenirs.

Out came our eight sleeping bags, eight satchels, cooler, medicine chest, martini shaker, mandolin, the spare tires and box of fan belts, lug wrench, and other tools. From under one seat, Mom pulled a box of paperbacks, crossword puzzle books, and the true crime magazines Gram enjoyed. Three aluminum lounge chairs, our camp stove, and another couple of boxes full of cheap silverware, plastic plates, and paper towels added to the heap.

What was the poor man to think of the fur coat and ball gowns that a relative gave Phyllis back on the East Coast? A wire contraption, Mom explained, was for stretching wool socks, a gift to us from a neighbor of Uncle Sal's in Florida. "She thought we could use them in Alaska," Mom said, "and she wasn't planning to live anywhere cold again so didn't need them."

A crowd gathered as we unloaded what looked like two van-loads of contents from the Wayward Bus. Tourists and truck drivers pointed and smirked, perhaps taking bets on whether it would all fit back in again.

The agent kept returning to the wine bottle, and finally Phyllis said, "Do you want to taste it?" She pulled the stopper out and reached for a cup.

The agent leaned over and sniffed, then grimaced. "No, you can close it up."

Two hours later, we paid five dollars in duty and left Mexico behind.

✧ ✧ ✧

The worst part about taking the wrong road, the punishment for the error, was having to drive across Texas—again! We spent the first night in Del Rio, where by ten the temperature cooled to eighty-one degrees. A weather report on the television in our motel room said Anchorage's temperature reached sixty degrees. That sounded heavenly. I caught a huge frog that evening, so big I couldn't hold it in one hand. The small frogs in Alaska—which is home to only two types of frog and one toad—reached a maximum or four or five inches long, so I couldn't resist carrying that big frog around to show Mom, Phyllis, and Gram before I let him go.

Late the next afternoon we pulled into Balmorhea State Park, a campground surrounded by sagebrush and sand, boasting the world's largest walled swimming pool. The pool, filled with murky greenish water, was surrounded by concrete too hot for bare feet. I kicked off one flip-flop to dip my toes into the cool water, until I noticed a turtle and then a fish in the water. Other people paddled and splashed in it, but I declined after seeing those critters.

Another family at the pool noticed our Alaska license plates and struck up a conversation with Mom. They recently left Alaska, after a three-year stint in the military at Eielson Air Force Base near Fairbanks. Finally, someone who knew our home state, people who could imagine the culture shocks we experienced as we traveled our own country. Mom enjoyed a long chat with them.

Carport-style roofs shaded the widely-spaced camping spots. We kids wandered around, bored out of our skulls and hoping the night would cool off. A few lizards scampered away from us. Finally we returned to our camp, kicking the sand from our flip-flops, and spread towels on the benches of the picnic table so the backs of our legs wouldn't burn.

Another family moved into the campsite nearest to ours, and their dog loped over to investigate us but before long shuffled back to the shade and his own water and food dishes. We picked at dinner, our appetites sapped by the heat.

"Girls, help us clean up, and we'll rinse off in a cool shower to help us sleep." Mom tried to encourage us out of our funks as darkness deepened around us. Crickets and frogs began their nighttime serenade, accompanied by the hum of an occasional passing car on the highway.

With a flashlight, we walked to the dingy shower building. As we approached, the light showing through a couple of high windows highlighted a collection of insects plastered against the screens, drawn to the bulbs inside.

I shuddered and pulled Mom's arm. "Look."

She paused, and with a sigh said, "They're on the outside. Come on, we'll be quick."

The shower helped, and after we all bedded down, most sleeping, the neighbors' dog ran by, whining.

From their campsite, scuffling erupted, then stage whispers. "Get out. Oh, God, that smell."

One sniff told me their dog met a skunk, and ended up the worse for it. The smell permeated our camp, too. I buried my face in the pillow, muttering my own complaints, and tried to sleep.

Gram fixed breakfast the next morning. Suddenly Mom's voice rose with a tone of warning.

"Mama, something's there next to you. Back away from it!"

Gram paid little attention.

"Mama!"

Finally, she looked around. "Oh, that little thing?" She picked up a Kleenex and squished the creature between her fingers, then tossed it aside.

It was a scorpion. She killed a scorpion with her bare hands and a tissue.

Gram was practically indestructible. I think her fearlessness reflected part confidence and part ignorance. Gram's education ended at the eighth-grade. Her mother never learned to speak English though she lived in America more than forty years.

When Grandpa found a job with the Alaska Railroad in 1945, he expected to go north alone and send money back to the family in New York, as he did previously when he worked in Greenland, Bermuda, and other places.

Gram didn't want to be left behind again and told him so. He started his job in Alaska several weeks before the family traveled north, and found Gram a job as a cook for the railroad maintenance crew he managed. She packed up the seven kids, and not much more than they could carry in paper bags and flimsy suitcases. At Grand Central Station they boarded a train, crossing the country to Seattle with only a few dollars and steamship tickets to Alaska.

In Moose Pass, they rented a house. Phyllis, age eighteen, took over parenting duties for her six siblings, while Gram went with Grandpa, ten miles up the track to Grandview: a few rough buildings owned by the railroad, with rails in either direction, surrounded by mountains and wilderness. Gram cooked for the half-dozen men who worked there and kept a black Lab for company.

One day in the kitchen, Gram called Blackie's name through the back door and held a bone out for him as she stirred something on the stove. She felt moist breath on her hand. Then Blackie sauntered in from the next room, bristling. She snapped her head around to see a black bear at the door, gnawing the dog's bone. She'd just hand-fed a bear.

As we crossed Texas, newspaper headlines carried more grim news of Vietnam: A fully loaded B-52 bomber crashed on the streets of a town north of Saigon, killing its crew and dozens of Vietnamese in a fiery explosion of two of the bombs it carried; Congress speculated whether the troop buildup was adequate; the Viet Cong pinned down an American unit; and Lackland Air Force Base braced for a doubling of the number of trainees preparing for military service.

Other headlines focused on the big civil rights news: President Johnson signed the new voting rights bill August 6. Federal registrars prepared to begin registering voters in states with discriminatory practices, and the Justice Department planned to file suit against Texas, Virginia, and Alabama, challenging the poll taxes they imposed in state elections. Such taxes for federal elections had been done away with in 1964. An article in the *Bryan (Texas) Daily Eagle* quoted Dr. Martin Luther King Jr. as saying his workers expected to register more than 900,000 Negro voters by the end of the month. More than 1,000 registered the first day.

Back home, two Soviet Russian mine workers made the news, landing near the coastal village of

Wales, Alaska, August 7. They drifted off course in their walrus skin boat while on a mushroom hunting trip in Siberia, seventy miles away. Both men initially said they wanted to return to Russia. After being picked up by the Coast Guard, they decided to request asylum in the U.S. Eventually, after several months, both of them changed their minds again and returned to Russia. They were not named on the official lists of Soviet-era defectors.

In the prior five years several KGB agents, scientists, and soldiers from Soviet Bloc nations defected to the West, a total of more than a dozen people who risked their lives to leave their countries. In our travels, we had entered and exited Canada and Mexico with only slight inconvenience. The true defectors garnered more news coverage than a couple of laborers who drifted into American territory by accident.

Chapter 21

SPEEDING WEST across the New Mexico desert, we zipped past a billboard advertising cactus milkshakes. Any kind of milkshake sounded cool and refreshing. But cactus? We had seen prickly pear cactus farms in Mexico. Since prickly pears grew on farms, we assumed it must be good to eat, but after Mom's misadventure trying to pick some for Gram, we avoided them. Now we decided to give it a try.

With more curiosity than confidence, we bought just one, then returned to the road and passed the shake around in the car, letting each person taste the frosty slush.

Turns out, a sip was more than enough. The cold drink we hoped would refresh us tasted so awful no one wanted a second sip. Finally, as the whole thing melted to soup in its waxy cup, one of us flung the contents out the window.

That cactus milkshake didn't go far. Most of it sprayed along the side of the van, and baked there, reminding us of the nasty taste for the next week or so. We finally scrubbed off the residue somewhere in California.

On August 6 we traveled Highway 380, Billy the Kid Trail, partway across New Mexico, and camped at Lincoln, Billy's hometown. Several signs warned "Watch for Rattlesnakes." We shared our anxiety with a family camping near us.

"Our thirteen-year-old son was bitten by a rattler five years ago," the man said.

"Is he okay?" Mom asked.

"He's playing right over there," he said, pointing to a kid talking with Glenn. "He lost three fingers."

"In spite of getting him to a doctor within twenty minutes," the boy's mother added.

Why in the big wide world had they come camping here in rattlesnake heaven?

Phyllis told Bill about the boy. *"No one will ever convince me that those bloody snakes won't kill me!"*

We zoomed across New Mexico, stopping along Highway 60 near Socorro to snap a photo of our van parked by the sign marking the continental divide, at 7,796 feet elevation. Mom, Marlie, and I leaned against the van, while Glenn and Jim propped against the sign in the baking sun. Phyllis's letter the day before noted the temperature of 106 degrees.

Today I wouldn't dream of driving across the southwest in summer without air conditioning, but we never considered such a luxury in 1965. After all, who would buy an air-conditioned car in Alaska? Movie stars and oil barons might drive air-conditioned cars, but not us.

The first automobile air conditioners were installed in limousines and luxury cars in New York in 1933. Packard, Chrysler, and Cadillac tried AC as an added option in the 1930s and 1940s. Interest grew, but the price was prohibitive for many buyers. In the early 1950s a car cost $1,500 to $3,000. Air conditioning added $350 to $500.

By 1960, only 20 percent of cars in the U.S. featured air conditioning. Today it is nearly universal in America, including cars sold in Alaska.

One attempt to mitigate the heat helped somewhat. We bought three seat pads with coils inside that allowed air flow beneath us. Loose-woven plastic covered the coils and didn't stick to sweaty skin. The three pads remained in the front seat, for the benefit of the driver and navigators.

Not far from Billy the Kid country, we drove through Capitan, New Mexico, where fifteen years earlier, a little bear cub with his paws badly burned was rescued from a forest fire. Nicknamed Smokey Bear, he was already famous when we drove through. An ad campaign in the early 1940s created Smokey Bear as the national mascot for fire safety in the outdoors. The rescued bear cub became a living symbol of the mascot and spent most of his life at the National Zoo in Washington, D.C.

Marlie's screams brought Mom flying to the bathroom of one desert campground. Marlie huddled against the far wall, gaping at a dozen or more four-inch grasshoppers flitting around the lights above the sink. Each time she started to move, another terrifying creature leapt across her path, preventing her escape until Mom rescued her.

"It's like being inside a science fiction comic book every night when we light the lantern," Mom wrote, because of all the bugs it attracted, insects of shocking size, variety, and ugliness.

We slowed our pace a bit in Arizona to visit the Petrified Forest, the Painted Desert, and the Grand

Canyon. I marveled at the logs of stone and the hills streaked with a dozen shades of red, brown, and gray, so much more vivid and awe-inspiring than the magazine photos I had seen.

By the time we reached the Grand Canyon late in the day August 8, campgrounds already filled to overflowing. We finally found a spot and crawled into bed about midnight. To our great delight, the nighttime temperature cooled so much that we actually slept in our sleeping bags again.

The next day we saw the canyon from several viewpoints, gaping in wonder at the colors, the depth, and the distance to the other side. We also checked out license plates throughout the park, but as usual, found none from Alaska. We had not seen any since May, in western Canada.

Late that afternoon we followed Route 66, brought to fame in a 1940s song and covered by the Rolling Stones in 1964. We hummed the tune as we headed to California. Interstate 40 was in the planning stages and would supplant Route 66 completely by the mid-1980s.

In Needles, California, the average high temperature between June 1 and mid-September is more than 100 degrees. Every. Miserable. Day. In early August, closer to 110. That's where we dragged in, late on an August evening, to spend the night. We had already eaten dinner—although the heat killed our appetites—and parked at the edge of a paved and lighted lot bordering the Colorado River.

We set up camp and walked to the restroom building to wash up. In the nimbus around each of the tall streetlights, insects large and small buzzed and fluttered. Bugs clogged window screens in the washhouse. I shuddered at the sight of them, and screamed when they flew by, sure man-eating creatures stalked me.

We ran back to the van, doused flashlights and lanterns, and hoped the insects wouldn't invade our sleeping space. Sweating on top of our sleeping bags, we listening to the drone of bugs and the gentle lapping of the Colorado River wandering to the sea. Maybe the little kids thought about Disneyland, our next destination, but geology and ancient ecosystems filled my mind. How could this peaceful, slow-moving river be the same one that cut through a mile of earth to form the Grand Canyon? What changed a forest of trees into stone?

After tossing and turning, Jim left our pallet at the back of the van. A terrible heat rash covered his back and legs.

When he didn't return, I climbed out and searched for him. At the bank of the river, he and my mom lay with their legs in the water, talking softly. I joined them. With the warm ground at our backs and dark waters flowing over our legs, we gradually cooled off enough to sleep a little.

The last desert of our journey awaited. We broke camp the next morning for one more day of driving before we reached the Pacific and turned our noses north toward home.

As we approached the West Coast, my goal changed. Eagerness for home replaced my wanderlust. Back in May, I happily left Alaska before school ended, and figured if we missed a few days in the fall, who cared? Now I wanted desperately to be home when school started again in three weeks. The other kids also wanted to be home, though perhaps not back in school. All eight of us were ready to vacate the Wayward Bus.

As we baked in the oven of the southwestern desert that week, NBC Sports aired its first telecast, a preseason game between the Buffalo Bills and Boston Patriots. Buffalo won 23-0. The five-year television contract, thus begun, ensured the viability of the American Football League.

President Johnson signed into law the Housing and Urban Development Act, which provided rent subsidies to the elderly and disabled, housing rehabilitation help for poor homeowners, and low down payment loans for veterans, among other provisions.

The Source by James Michener—a favorite author of mine—topped the New York Times bestseller list for fiction, beginning July 11 and remaining there until May 1966. Theodore White's *The Making of the President 1964*, recounting Lyndon Johnson's re-election battle with Barry Goldwater, topped the nonfiction list.

Chapter 22

WE FOUND A CAMPGROUND near Anaheim and chattered through the evening about the Magic Kingdom.

Among photos from the Drive are fourteen pictures taken at Disneyland. In fuzzy color pictures, we captured Sleeping Beauty's Castle, a pirate ship, and whirling teacups. They show some of our fun that day. In one photo, Gram poses with the white rabbit from Alice in Wonderland. After the Matterhorn bobsled ride, I wrote to Dad: *"Glenn was disgusted because Marlie and Mom and I were screaming."*

My favorite Disney character was Flower the Skunk, and Mom talked me into posing next to him (or is it her?) for a photo that day. My oldest childhood toy is a stuffed animal of Flower, ratty and threadbare now. My Flower would never pass muster as a toy today: a thick metal wire pokes through the tail and the plastic eyes could pop off and choke a child.

Flower befriended Bambi in the classic 1947 Disney film. Back then, before people could easily own a copy of almost any movie, the studios re-released older movies in theaters every so often, and *Bambi* appeared for the second time in 1957, when I was five. That's the year we moved from Moose Pass to Anchorage, and it is one of the first movies I ever watched on the big screen.

Why would a skunk character appeal to me so much? Maybe it was the novelty—Alaska is the only state with no skunks. Nor does it want them, I might add. It's illegal to import, sell, or breed them there, and the state can exterminate any they find.

There I stood in Disneyland, next to my movie hero, a six-foot-tall skunk.

Disneyland celebrated it tenth anniversary in 1965 and called its celebration a "Tencennial." Disney planned all sorts of expansion in the Magic Kingdom. The park already boasted the first daily passenger-carrying monorail in America, and the sternwheeler *Mark Twain* plied a manmade river. We visited a pirate ship, but the Blue Bayou and Pirates of the Caribbean were still being developed. Before its installation in the park, much of It's a Small World was already on display at the World's Fair in New York. We recognized Disneyland's newest character that year, Mary Poppins, having seen the movie during our stop in Virginia.

The park was much smaller in 1965 than it is today. Tokyo, Paris, and Hong Kong had not yet dreamed of having Magic Kingdoms of their own. And we were not aware—hardly anyone was—that Walt Disney was very busy that year buying forty-three square miles of land in central Florida through a variety of dummy corporations as the site for a much larger theme park, which would become Walt Disney World.

Disney built his life on animations and fantasies, beginning in his late teens as a student at Kansas City Art Institute. In his twenties, he produced hundreds of popular animated short comedies and created the character of Mickey Mouse. In 1932 he created the first cartoon to win an Oscar. By the time he opened Disneyland in Anaheim in 1955, Walt Disney was a world-renowned filmmaker. His Florida dreams did not come true during his lifetime, however. Disney died in late 1966.

My letter to Dad noted my unexpected discovery that Peter Pan, in Disneyland at least, was a girl. In addition, *"we were charged by elephants, hippos, rhinos, and all other things that charge at Disneyland (mainly the ticket booths). We saw a safari in a tree with animals and vultures waiting 'til they fell down. We saw Swiss Family Robinson's tree house with running water in almost every room. There was a sink made from the shell of a giant clam."*

The Swiss Family Robinson Treehouse at Disneyland closed in March 1999 and was redeveloped as Tarzan's Treehouse in time for the summer crowds that year. The Swiss Family Robinson theme continues at three other Disney parks.

An entertainment calendar on the back of a 1965 Disneyland brochure shows that during the week of our visit, the Duke Ellington Orchestra played most evenings. We didn't stay late enough to hear them, though.

The attention to detail throughout the park impressed Mom the most. *"It's every storybook and every adventure you ever read about from the time you were old enough to read, all brought to life in a very magnificent personal sort of way and you can't help but love Mr. Disney even as you walk away with aching feet and empty wallet. If only you could have been there with me today to share the shine in the kids' eyes!"*

Mom's letter notes that *"we just had a wonderful grand time with our last $50"* and that we had just enough money left to return home.

Fifty dollars for eight people to enjoy a grand time at Disneyland? A bright red brochure titled "Two Wonderful Ways to Enjoy Disneyland" outlines the price structure at the time. One option, a guided tour with an "attractive Disneyland Tour Guide" for two hours, visiting all four lands in the Magic Kingdom, cost five dollars per adult and three dollars for children under twelve. The second option was a ticket book special, with either ten or fifteen tickets. The Big Ten ticket book cost four dollars for adults, $3.50 for juniors (twelve to seventeen), and three dollars for children (three to eleven). So for twenty-eight dollars all of us could explore the park, with two or three dollars each to spend on food and souvenirs. An upgrade to the Deluxe Fifteen ticket book would add a dollar per person.

How does that compare to today's prices? In the summer of 2018, on a midweek day in mid-August, our group of eight would have paid more than nine hundred dollars just for park admission.

Other entertainment also cost a lot less in 1965. Orchestra level seats for a Broadway show cost less than ten dollars, and balcony seats, less than five. Admission to movie theaters averaged a dollar. Tickets for a Friday afternoon Beatles concert in Chicago sold for $5.50, about the same as a professional baseball game at the time.

We splurged on the visit to Disneyland, leaving foot-weary but happy at the end of the day.

Chapter 23

WHILE WE DRAGGED OUR TIRED BODIES out of Disneyland August 11, 1965, about twenty-five miles away in Los Angeles, a traffic stop turned ugly when a California Highway Patrolman arrested a young black man, Marquette Frye, for reckless driving. Frye's brother, who was a passenger in the car, and his mother, who lived nearby, were both arrested along with Marquette after a fight broke out with the police.

Oblivious to all this, we focused on finding our way across Los Angeles's unfamiliar landscape.

As we watched the performing animals at Marineland August 12, meetings held in Los Angeles attempted to calm the unrest building throughout the previous night. The car radio distracted the drivers, so we kept it off while driving through the city, so heard none of the news. After a quick stop at a market on our way to Ventura that night, we set up camp on the beach.

The next day, Phyllis wrote to Bill: *"Winnie and Ma took the car into town for to do the laundry and supplies and mail. Wish we were set up to stay another day or 2. It's just lovely. The old Pacific is out there pounding away."*

As Mom and Gram thumbed through old magazines while the laundry dried that day, August 13, a woman burst through the doors of the laundromat, near hysterical. "Oh my God," she screamed, and grabbed Gram by the shoulders, shaking her. "The n——rs are burning down the city! You better get outta here! They're killing people."

Mom strode over and said, "Take your hands off my mother!" The woman shared her news with a more receptive audience, while Mom and Gram gathered their laundry—some of it not yet dry—and headed back to the beach.

Yes, flames devoured parts of Watts amid the boiling racial tensions. That laundromat announcement in Ventura was the first we'd heard of it. We were already well away from the unrest but apparently not far enough for some people.

As I read through the letters Mom and Phyllis sent home, once again I realized how much they left out when they shared their news with Dad and Uncle Bill. Why was this never recorded in a letter home? Mom returned from the laundromat shaken—far more by the woman's behavior than any sense of threat from riots. The story has been told time and again over the years.

Mom wrote letters to Dad August 14 and August 15, neither saying a word about the laundromat encounter or the riots in Watts. Just news about our stay at Ventura beach: *"The ocean water is really cold—about 70 degrees but sure felt good. Did a little surfing and boy that's fun!"* She mentions visiting the mother of an Alaskan friend and lets homesickness bleed through: *"I was so disappointed as there was no mail from you, or the brochures on the ferry system, but I'm sure Troyce [a co-worker of Mom's at SeaLand] will have word from you. That's why we decided to wait for her plane."* Mom wrote that letter in the coffee shop at Santa Barbara airport. She continued: *"As we've traveled up the coast of California the countryside gets prettier. It's still not very green but with the beautiful blue Pacific stretching out from the foothills it's cool and lovely. The homes along the ocean are out of this world. (Priced about the same as Anchorage) Incidentally, carpenters (we hear) make $6 per hour down here. I'm not sure I believe it!"*

Minimum wage at the time was $1.25 per hour, and median annual income for a family was $6,900. No wonder six dollars an hour sounded unbelievable.

Mom continued the letter later that day: *"Well it was sure good to talk to Troyce for a few minutes. Still no mail tho—guess you must be busy, but we'll surely hear from you at Reedsport."*

Seeing Troyce and several other Alaskan friends we connected with on our way up the West Coast stoked the homesickness in Mom and Phyllis.

We kids were homesick as well as tired of being cooped up in the car, after more than twelve weeks of mostly camping or sleeping on floors and sofas. Gram remained her calm and patient self, pursing her lips when Mom and Phyllis snapped at each other but always willing to trade seats or play cards.

"North to Alaska" became our theme song driving up the west coast, with just a few more stops to visit friends.

Mom's letter August 15 tells about the next one: *"Don't know if I told you the other day down in L.A. we met a gal at a supermarket who wanted us to* come spend the nite with her and her family. We were flabbergasted! A complete stranger. So as not to hurt her feelings we took down her phone number and address, telling her we had friends to meet in Ventura. Well, it seems she had another home in Santa Barbara just 30 miles north of Ventura and would we please stop and just have dinner... We decided to call this nut just for a lark. Well, we went out to her house and they are really one of those rare type just wonderful people. She is from Canada and that's one of the reasons she's so interested in talking to people from Alaska. She's a teacher and her husband is a Physics professor at UC Santa Barbara. They have two daughters. One is grown and wasn't there. The other is just Sandy's age and in the 10th grade, having skipped two grades. They had a big roast chicken dinner waiting for us, a fantastic spread with delicious dessert and wine. They have a big odd looking Lyle Reed type house, which they built themselves (unheard of down here). It's not quite finished you know but is very comfortable."

I remember the spacious rooms in that house, and the light switches which, rather than being placed near the doorways, were set in the middle of the wall somewhere, not easy to find unless you knew where to look.

Phyllis wrote to Bill about our visit too: "They have been to Europe on the same kind of trip as we are doing now. They took a boat to Paris, rented an apartment for a month, bought a secondhand car and got to know Paris like a book, then took off and traveled thru France, Italy, Germany, England and Scotland, etc. They stayed in these "youth hostels" which are or were abandoned castles or buildings that *this travelers' club has taken over. You can stay in them for 30 cents a night or some such price. Do you remember reading about this? Anyway they figured that was the best way to travel because they met so many interesting people from all over etc. Maybe you and I can do it?"*

Reading this letter, I can't help but wonder, did Phyllis even know the man she married? Uncle Bill in a youth hostel?? To use a phrase common to my parents when they heard something they couldn't imagine, I've got a four-wheel picture of Uncle Bill in a youth hostel. Though he and Phyllis traveled more than my parents did, making a few road trips down the Alcan to the Lower 48, he was far more the Motel 6 kind of guy than one who would bunk with strangers in a hostel. The gregarious and adventuresome inclinations of Phyllis and Mom caused chagrin, not inspiration, for both Uncle Bill and my dad.

Professor Hall and his wife plied us with questions throughout dinner and convinced us to spend the night. That evening they treated us to a festival of music and dance celebrating the founding of Santa Barbara—which included some of the same dances we saw at the Ballet Folklorico in Mexico City. This surprised me, bending my mind to the truth that California once belonged to Mexico.

We returned to their house about 11 p.m. and Phyllis wrote: *"We slept all over the living room floor and talked til 1:30 or so. Got up about 8:30 ... and got out of there at noon. They are fantastic people in their hospitality. We felt as tho we had known them all our lives and that the house was ours. I made a suggestion, sort of, to Mrs. Hall that maybe when they come to Alaska if he were going to teach at a summer session in Anchorage, they could live in our house and we would use their beach house in L.A. for a vacation. She really liked the idea so maybe in a couple of years we can take a long rest on a beach in L.A. How about that? I can hear you cussin' and raving, but it is still a good idea."*

Yes, I can imagine him cussing and grumbling about it even now. I'm not sure how long Phyllis or Mom stayed in touch with the Halls, but no such home exchange ever materialized.

By this time, we had read newspaper accounts and seen the rioting in Watts on television. Over the next few days the friends we visited joked with us about whether we started the riots as we drove through L.A. and then left town on the run. I knew, though, that the burning buildings and angry people were not a joke.

Headlines about Watts filled the papers: "Rioting, Death Reign in LA"; "Riot Death Toll Reaches 22"; "Curfew in LA Defied"; and the long-lived slogan, quoted in bold print, "Burn, Baby, Burn." Rioters chanted that slogan as arson fires destroyed $40 million in property.

News of Vietnam was pushed off many front pages, especially in California papers, but deeper in the paper stories of North Vietnam's growing air power appeared. Military reconnaissance photos of missile sites in North Vietnam appeared in newspapers across America.

The war in Vietnam wasn't the only conflict in the world. While border clashes between India and Pakistan escalated, South Korea approved a controversial peace treaty with Japan. The United States and the Congo Republic closed their embassies due to alleged mistreatment of American diplomatic staff. Guatemala was engaged in a civil war that would last another thirty years. Mozambique battled for independence from Portugal, an effort that finally succeeded ten years later.

And from the social pages, the Matrix night club in San Francisco opened that week with the first-ever performance by Jefferson Airplane. Lead singer Marty Balin, who co-owned the club, pulled a group of musicians together to explore the emerging folk-rock music style. They became pioneers in psychedelic rock. Their first album debuted in 1967, and the band dissolved in 1972, leaving behind a body of legendary rock-era music.

Chapter 24

UP THE PACIFIC COAST ON HIGHWAY 1, we found a campground at Big Sur for two dollars for the night of August 15. Pictures of the Big Sur area usually focus on the rugged coastline with crashing waves at the base of rocky cliffs.

These scenes did not impress me much. Alaska specialized in rugged country. We prided ourselves on having the biggest mountains on the continent, more coastline than all the other states combined, with very little of it inhabited. Wild beasts populated millions of square miles of Alaskan wilderness. How could the ruggedness of Big Sur impress me?

But the trees were another story. That forest of tall, straight, magnificent redwoods, some big enough to drive a car through, mesmerized me. People often think of Alaska as having big trees, and in some places that's true. Not where I grew up. So we camped among the giant redwoods and explored, looking up from the mossy forest floor through the branches soaring overhead, and played hide-and-seek among the massive trunks. The next morning as we cleaned up after breakfast, Glenn took a hike nearby. He leaned against a tree to evaluate the scope of the forest surrounding him. Near his feet, a swarm of stinging insects emerged from a hole, disturbed in their ground-nest, and rose up around his legs.

He raced back toward the camp, running through a creek rather than over the bridge, in hopes of losing some of them, and howling from the stings. Mom swatted and waved a towel, dispersing the attackers and calming Glenn.

We gathered around to encourage him, holding cold wet washcloths on his stings. That ended our forest explorations. We realized that we didn't understand the dangers around us. Glenn calmed down and fell asleep, which wasn't really a good sign.

Mom wrote to Dad the next day: *"He was covered with bees and was quite hysterical. Well it may look funny in the movies but can be quite serious as we've learned. We didn't take him to a Dr. as there was none about, just had him hold ice on his numerous bites. He slept all morning in the car, felt good this afternoon in San Francisco where we toured through Chinatown and Fisherman's Wharf and had a big seafood dinner. But tonight the calf of one leg is numb and a little paralyzed. He has no feeling in it. His legs are both real sore and of course he is limping terribly, but I'm sure he'll be fine by morning."*

Living in Alaska, where home remedies and "wait-and-see" provided the first line of defense for medical needs, gave Mom strong confidence in Glenn's well-being. Poor Glenn! His body battled a powerful toxin from wasp stings, not "bee bites" as she described them.

His legs, shaking at first, gradually regained their feeling and function, but his encounter with a ground hive of wasps defined my memories of Big Sur, even more than the giant trees surrounding us. Alaska's insect population of mosquitos and "no-see-'ems" ill-prepared us for the tarantulas, scorpions, and wasps we encountered on the Drive. The encounter added one more good reason I wanted to race home: fleeing from these dangers.

Writing to Dad, Mom mentions a collection of matchbooks she gathered as we traveled. *"You'll have lots of interesting times lighting cigarettes. I'd have mailed them home 'cept it is agin the law."* Fast forward to 2007 when we cleaned out Aunt Phyllis's house in Coulee City, Washington, for her move to assisted living. Among her many collectibles—hundreds of coffee mugs and a large spoon collection—I found old stashes of matchbooks. I wish now that I had paid more attention and kept some of them. I suspect she saved them from the Drive in '65.

Among the ephemera in the Drive archives is a stained and spattered brochure from San Martin Winery in the San Jose area. We stopped there on our way to San Francisco. One side of the flyer contains a printed list of wines, with notes in Phyllis's handwriting about varieties she tried: Sylvaner Riesling "Rhine wine—dry"; Hostess Emerald Riesling "too sweet!"; and on through three reds, a champagne, crème sherry, and some berry wines. She starred the Cabernet Sauvignon, apparently her favorite—and one of the more expensive offerings—selling for $1.99 a bottle or $21.49 a case. The berry wines, on the low end, cost $1.29 each, and a bottle of San Martin brandy would set you back $4.60.

Later in life Phyllis developed a taste for crème sherry and enjoyed a tot every evening for many years.

Back to Mom's letter of August 16: *"Tonight we are in San Rafael just a little way from Frisco. The Golden*

Gate Bridge isn't golden—It's orange, and it is so short! I thought it would be at least a mile long. I'm so dumb. And Alcatraz! It's so close, looks like it would be a cinch to swim to the mainland but guess it isn't."

I stared at Alcatraz as we passed, still thinking of it as the iconic national prison, since it closed only two years earlier. In cop and courtroom television shows, the threat to the bad guys was often imprisonment at Alcatraz, where America's most violent and troublesome prisoners were sent between 1934 and 1963, when deteriorating buildings and operational costs led to its closure.

Although thirty-six prisoners attempted escapes in its twenty-nine years of operation, the penitentiary claims that all attempts failed. However, five were never accounted for and are listed as "missing and presumed drowned." But what really became of them? It looked to me, as it did to Mom, like some could have escaped.

Today Alcatraz is a National Historic Landmark, home to various art installations and the site of Native American ceremonies.

In San Rafael we visited the Doyles, friends of Gram's, and their reaction echoed what we had heard from others on our travels: Mom and Phyllis were so *brave* and *wonderful* to make this journey. What courage they demonstrated, traveling so far from home without any men along.

This reaction seemed odd to me. My family lived a two-hour drive from most of our relatives, a drive both Mom and Phyl made on their own many times. They both knew how to change a flat tire and diagnose basics like a broken fan belt or a radiator needing water. Each day of our trip, they just drove the van to our next destination. If we wanted to see

Cape Cod or the Grand Canyon, we followed roads to find our way there.

As I digested these comments, I realized Mom and Phyllis demonstrated a real fearlessness by embarking on our journey of discovery. They ignored the mockers and doubters, worked hard to earn money for the trip, and found creative ways around the greater obstacles women faced fifty years ago.

Or, perhaps, their desire to show us the world outweighed whatever fears they had.

Mom's letter continues, *"San Francisco is the prettiest city we've been in. I really wouldn't mind living here (someday). Right now I just want to be home in Anchorage—soon!"*

Mom wasn't the only one who wanted to be home. In Phyllis's letter that day, she says: *"We are stopped at Santa Rosa, visiting Richard Steel. Jimmy feels as tho he has come home, and doesn't want to leave— tho two hours ago he was ready to drive day & night to get back to Alaska. I sure am anxious to get down the road tho. Sure wish we had enuf money left, I'd let him fly home. Maybe Harold [Jim's dad] will have some. Probably not tho."*

Richard Steel, the son of our close family friend Allan Steel, had lived in Alaska with his dad, just a few blocks from our house, when the earthquake struck in 1964. The Steels' house sustained more damage than ours, and for a few weeks Richard and Allen bunked at our place. A couple of years older than I, about Jim's age, Richard cared little for an awkward sixth-grader. I lived in awe of him and Jim, though in fact they were simply awkward eighth-graders themselves. Soon after the earthquake, when Phyllis's family moved to Anchorage, Richard and Jim became friends. Some of their buddies owned motorcycles—I recall one guy we named "Suzuki Ray"—who occasionally condescended to give us younger girls a thrilling ride around the block.

While Richard lived at our house, he and I found little in common. We bickered, snapped, and huffed about each other most of the time. But one thing drew us together every night at 6 p.m.—the "Coke Show" on the radio, a call-in request program broadcast from a rooftop studio at the Bun Drive-In, an icon of 1960s Anchorage. Richard and I sprawled on the two bunkbeds in the room he shared with Glenn and closed out the rest of the household while we listened to rock and roll and the radio banter of Ron Moore, who called himself The Royal Coachman.

In that hour, Richard and I coexisted peacefully, united against anyone who might interrupt the music. Oh, we still had our differences: Richard loved Elvis, and I was not (yet) a fan. But we mellowed out together listening to the Beatles, the Supremes, Herman's Hermits, and the Beach Boys. Older teens in Anchorage—the social elite in miniskirts and white knee-high boots, and jocks in letterman jackets—would drive to the Bun in their Ford Mustangs or Pontiac GTOs and rev the engines, waiting for a waitress to collect their orders. I only dreamed of that kind of fun, while Richard and I listened to the dedications, the latest music, and the closing song each night, "Earth Angel."

Before school started in the fall of 1964, Richard returned to California to live with his mother. In August 1965, nearly a year later, we stopped to see him in Santa Rosa.

Mom wrote to Dad August 16: *"We picked up a passenger in Santa Rosa. (Don't panic.) We are taking him only as far as Seattle to visit Allan's mom. Richard is now 6' tall and still weighs the same as he did. (What a sight!) He's beside himself with joy at being able to go to Seattle with us. He really wouldn't go back to Alaska anyway but was happy to see us all!"*

Phyllis wrote to Bill the same day: *"We will camp tonight near Leggett and probably make Reedsport late tomorrow. So will write again after we leave there. I am hoping that we get into Anchorage on a Thursday or Friday so you will drive to Moose Pass with us to get rid of a bunch of the stuff. I'll drive if you want so you can rest Saturday. Why don't you just get sick that weekend? You could get sick and go back to work Monday night! Huh, please??*

"Love, Phyl"

From our campsite in Leggett, Mom wrote: *"Glenn's leg is fine now and all his 'stings' are gone. Poor little guy sure was miserable. We are in Giant Redwood country. Man these trees are, like, big. There's a whole house in one log (made like a trailer house—very cute!)."*

Yes, more big trees surrounded us, but after Glenn's wasp incident, I approached them cautiously. The curiosities like the house crafted from a log, or the log you could drive through, amused all of us, but we didn't care to linger. My mind honed in on home, just a couple of weeks away, and starting school, where I could share my summer adventures with my friends and teachers.

Our plans included no more tourist attractions to slow our northern progress—we were bound for home, all equally eager but for different reasons. From Leggett, we drove 350 miles to Reedsport, Oregon, for a two-night stay with Moose Pass friends, Max and Sis Foster, who had retired there. Mom wrote: *"If there's no letter from you I'll just stay in*

Oregon this winter. I keep hoping maybe you're getting a little lonesome for us. (How's that for a little indulgence in self-pity.) Enuf!"

No doubt Dad worked long hours that summer. Alaska was rebuilding at top speed. But his failure to communicate stemmed from his character. Dad was an only child for more than eight years, until his brother arrived. He never lacked for affection, and his parents provided well for him. Mom's emotional neediness developed in childhood as she competed with six siblings in a household that was chronically broke. Her pursuit of Dad's attention and affection, a regular fixture in her letters, caused him to withdraw rather than respond with love and caring.

While we rested a couple of nights in Reedsport with the Fosters, Phyllis wrote to Bill: *"We got a letter from Allan Steel and it had a receipt for paid in full fare for everyone & car for the ferry so we will be coming home on the ferry."*

Though we all rejoiced at this news, other pressures flowed in the letter. *"You know how slow Reeds [my family] move even tho I'm constantly prodding and nagging. I always thought it was Lyle but it isn't. Anyway I'm so tense now waiting to get home I can hardly stand it. Will see you when we get there—probably won't write much more as it wouldn't get there before we do anyway. Will write just before we go into Canada so you'll know better when we'll be home."*

The stress affected everybody. And now we squeezed an extra person in the car—Richard Steel at six feet tall occupied more than his fair share of the limited space. But Jim's attitude improved a lot during the few days Richard rode with us, so including him proved worthwhile.

On August 21 we drove north again, through Portland and up to Aberdeen, where Jim's dad, Harold, worked, for a brief visit. The next day, a Sunday, we arrived in Seattle. We drove around Woodland Park looking for the location of an annual picnic for people from Seward, Alaska. When we finally arrived, the picnic was over, and someone was taking down the sign. Disappointed, Mom and Phyllis groused about missing the picnic as we drove around Lake Washington to the east side. We stayed with Allen Steel's mother—Richard's grandmother—in Kirkland, and several Alaskan friends stopped to visit with Mom, Phyllis, and Gram that evening.

We kids helped load the van Monday morning, while Mom visited SeaLand's Seattle office and met people she corresponded with at her job in Anchorage. A few of them had visited the Alaska office, and seeing them recharged her eagerness for home. Richard and Jim spent the morning together, sneaking away from us younger ones to smoke cigarettes and look at car magazines. Without Richard, the van would seem almost spacious. Antsy to leave, I calculated our remaining days of road travel and daydreamed of returning to school.

By midday Mom returned, and we pointed the Wayward Bus north. In a thousand miles we'd reach Prince Rupert, launching point for the ferry system called the Alaska Marine Highway taking us to Haines. School would start the following week in Anchorage, and we all counted the days. Two days' drive to Prince Rupert, two days on the ferry to Haines, and two days' drive to Anchorage.

During our hours in the car we wrote lyrics for another song about the trip, this one to the tune of the "Battle of New Orleans," a Billboard number one

hit for Johnny Horton in 1959. With apologies to
Horton and songwriter Jimmy Driftwood:

In 1965 we took a little drive
And it really is a miracle that we came back alive
We loaded down our Chevy bus
with all the proper gear
And headed down the Alcan, it was a thing to fear.

We shifted our gears and we passed another truck
There wasn't quite as many as there was a while ago
We shifted once more and trusted in our luck
And we prayed to heaven that a tire wouldn't blow.

We drove through the valleys
and we drove over mountains
And we drove over places that a Ford couldn't go.
We drove so fast that the cops couldn't catch us
All the way from Anchorage to the Gulf of Mexico.

We told our relations we would take 'em by surprise
But they could see us comin'
and we heard their mournful cries.
They tried to lock the doors
but we caught 'em in the act
So they grinned a little sickly
and they offered us a snack.

We drove through the Everglades
in the middle of the night
With the Seminoles and alligators givin' us a fright.
The temperature was 95 with mosquitos on parade
So we shifted into high gear and left the Everglades.

In the month of July down in Mobile Alabam'

An Arkansas traveler hit us with a wham.
His eyes bugged out when we said he'd have to pay
But we held our ground and
called the cops to see what they would say.

Two handsome cops pulled into sight
and we turned on the charm
And before you even knew it
we were talkin' arm in arm.
The Arkansas traveler might not have to pay,
But we sure had fun in Alabama
on that sunny day.

On the car radio, the hits kept playing. Herman's
Hermits reached the top spot with "I'm Henry VIII, I
Am," just four months after their number one hit,
"Mrs. Brown, You've Got a Lovely Daughter." Sonny
and Cher climbed to number one with "I Got You,
Babe." If we created new lyrics for these tunes, they
don't survive.

Chapter 25

G ENEROSITY DOGGED OUR STEPS all around the continent that summer. Live herbs from Gram's brother to spice up our meals, a fur coat for Alaskan winters from a great-aunt, a mandolin from Uncle Wayne in Wisconsin, and the gallon of vinegar that sparked suspicion in the customs inspector, the van filled fuller and fuller.

Perhaps one of the most generous acts, and one that didn't add weight to be hauled, was Allan Steel's purchase of our ferry tickets from Prince Rupert to Haines, saving us more than five hundred miles of further wear and tear on the Wayward Bus and cramped travel for all of us.

Dad, Mom, and Allan all worked in the transportation industry in Alaska during the 1960s. In addition to their professional friendship, he and my parents drank and played pinochle together. Allan developed an expertise at loading freighters and later in his career traveled to ports all over the world to assure that freight balanced correctly on cargo ships.

My brother, Glenn, was a great favorite of Allan's and remained so as long as Allan lived. About four years after the Drive, and well before Glenn could obtain a driver's license, Allan gave him an Amphicar. Germany manufactured these amphibious cars for only a few years in the early to mid-1960s. According to Wikipedia, one owner claimed, "It's not a good car and it's not a good boat, but it does just fine" largely because of modest performance in and out of water. Another added, "We like to think of it as the fastest car on the water and fastest boat on the road." A couple of years later when Glenn could drive, he discovered that the Amphicar required insurance as a sports car, in the same category as a Corvette, despite its maximum speed of seventy miles per hour.

Allan was generous to our family in other ways too. When he lived with us after the earthquake, he often witnessed sibling squabbles over doing the dishes. One day a delivery truck arrived at our house and delivered a brand new portable dishwasher—a gift from Allan. Our squabbles over washing dishes ended, and we began arguing about who would load the dishwasher.

Mom and Phyl considered the ferry option from our earliest days on the road, if our funds lasted long enough to do it. By the time we picked up Richard in Santa Rosa, we had spent most of our money. I can only imagine Mom's conversation with Allan as she arranged to drive Richard to Seattle. Did she talk about how the van limped along as we approached twenty thousand miles in three months of heavy travel? And our longing for home? Maybe she hinted at the growing tensions between her and Phyllis.

In any case, Allan bought us the ferry tickets.

The Alaska Marine Highway launched the MV *Malaspina* in early 1963, bringing the first connection for auto traffic to the isolated towns of Ketchikan, Juneau, and Skagway. From Prince Rupert, British Columbia, the southern terminus, travelers could use Canadian ferries, or the highway system, to travel farther south.

Today, the southern terminus is Bellingham, Washington. With ten ferries in service, routes stretch more than two thousand miles, from Dutch Harbor in southwest Alaska to Bellingham, serving thirty-five communities.

From Kirkland to Prince Rupert we drove through a different part of Canada than we saw coming south—*Beautiful British Columbia*, as license plates today proclaim. Rugged country, damp and green, with evergreens piercing the sky like cathedral spires as we bore north, ever north. It almost seems like we all leaned forward as we drove, urging the car toward home.

The Wayward Bus groaned and whined up the road, and with each new sound, Mom and Phyl exchanged anxious glances. Did our supplies include another spare fan belt? Was that scraping sound from our brakes? Would a breakdown cause us to miss the ferry? That night we stayed in a motel in Lac la Hache, British Columbia, where Mom wrote her final diary entry.

"Should reach Prince Rupert tomorrow. Dead tired right now and looking forward to the ferry ride. Thank God for the ferry."

Despite stops to check the belts, brakes, and other noisemakers in our rear-mounted engine, Mom and Phyllis coaxed the van into Prince Rupert in time. We enjoyed a couple of days cruising the Inside

Passage with room to roam—a welcome change from driving. Glassy waters, gray-green with glacial silt, reflected the soaring trees and rocky shoreline we passed. From the deck rail, I watched cars and trucks drive off and on the ferry at each stop, idly curious about the logistics of parking in the belly of the vessel. Between stops we shared the waterway with fishing boats.

The Inside Passage revealed to us a new part of Alaska, dense evergreen forests dropping to rocky shores, with isolated logging and fishing towns scattered among the islands. The protected waters, green and calm, differed sharply from Seward's choppy Resurrection Bay or Cook Inlet near Anchorage. Totem poles, cultural icons of the Tlingit and Haida peoples, welcomed us at the ferry towns. We'd learned about them in school, completely different cultures from the Athabascan and Alutiq, Yupic and Inupiat people from other parts of Alaska. Even though we were back in Alaska, we still discovered new things.

Phyllis and Mom fretted about a possible breakdown on our last leg, about seven hundred fifty miles from Haines to Anchorage. But they rested on the ferry to be ready for that last long haul. In her final letter to Bill from Kirkland, Phyllis mentioned her disappointment in missing the picnic in Seattle, which was to be a final event of the trip. *"Sure would have been nice. So now we'll just wind it up on the ferry. Maybe have a drink or two at the bar & throw the glass over the side. Would that be a proper toast? Or drink farewell to a well-spent summer?"*

They did enjoy that drink. The detailed list of expenses for the trip includes an entry for martinis on the ferry, costing $2.90.

We left the ferry in Haines and just drove. The route led us back into Canada, and in about four hours, we rejoined the Alcan Highway at Haines Junction. I don't remember stopping overnight on that stretch, we were all so focused on home, home, home. Many hours later, we began to see familiar territory, the northern outskirts of Anchorage, and then, at last, our own back yard.

Dad stood at the back door, transferred his beer can to his cigarette hand, and stepped out to give us each a hug. We grabbed our satchels, leaving the rest to be unloaded the next day, so Phyllis could drive the van to her house. Inside, the house still smelled of home, faded a bit due to Dad's absence half of each week. And in my own bedroom I had my white and gold French provincial twin bed, all to myself.

We had done it.

In those last days of August, Gemini V splashed down in the Atlantic, with astronauts Gordon Cooper and Pete Conrad glad, as we were, to leave their cramped vehicle behind. They spent almost eight days in space—the longest manned trip so far. The Soviet Union announced a new Soyuz initiative that they hoped would land their own man on the moon before America's Apollo program.

Public schools across the South opened to mandated desegregation, although one hundred seventy-two school districts opted to forgo federal funds rather than accept black students. Integration of schools has been a stubborn problem. In Mississippi, the NAACP filed a lawsuit in 1965 on behalf of black students in Cleveland School District, who make up nearly 70 percent of the student population. That lawsuit succeeded—but not until the fall of 2017. According to an Associated Press report, in 2014 forty-three desegregation lawsuits remained on the Justice Department's books. Desegregation is not just a Southern problem, either. Lawsuits continued late in 2018 in Hartford, Connecticut, and in New Jersey, in the pursuit of equal educational opportunities.

The death toll in Vietnam continued to climb, statistics we watched more and more closely in the coming years. More than fifty Marines died in Operation Starlight, the first U.S. Marine offensive and the first solely American operation of the war. A Gallup poll reported that 60 percent of Americans supported sending military troops to Vietnam. Mom was not one of them.

Chapter 26

SUCH A WELCOME SIGHT, home, after all those miles on the road! We appreciated the spaciousness of our house, the freedom to wander the neighborhood, and the companionship of friends we left behind in the spring. I had not received any letters from friends that summer.

School started a day or two after our return— barely time to unpack our bags and sort through the boxes of discount store school clothes Mom mailed home from Wisconsin in May.

I entered eighth grade at a different school, Central Junior High, due to boundary line adjustments in a rapidly growing school district. For the third time in less than two years, I started at a new school, leaving many of my old friends behind. Anchorage's population grew about 50 percent between 1960 and 1970.

Something fundamental shifted at home while we traveled that summer. Seams opened in the family like the cracks in Alaska's earth crust in

1964. The season apart changed Dad in ways I didn't recognize for years.

During nearly fourteen years of marriage to a woman he wed reluctantly, Dad coped by drinking too many beers, too many martinis. Mom, longing for attention since childhood, and finding less love than she needed from Dad, discovered community theatre in Anchorage about the time Marlie, Glenn, and I were all in elementary school. Through the early 1960s, she found the accolades there that Dad never provided at home. In her first role, she won a Best Supporting Actress award, and soon forged lifelong friendships in the theatre crowd.

Dad resented the late nights of rehearsal and didn't have much interest in live theatre. He poured himself into a business he started about 1960, Freight Service Company. They worked together publishing tariffs for trucking companies using a mimeograph machine that left bluish smudges on their hands and a chemical odor in their little rented office. They also audited freight bills to recover overcharges for clients who shipped goods to Alaska. Mom learned enough about freight and tariffs to secure the job at SeaLand in 1964.

From 1960 until the end of 1963, we lived in an unfinished basement off O'Malley Road. Today O'Malley is a major paved thoroughfare in the suburbs, but at that time the gravel road climbed into the foothills several miles south of Anchorage proper.

By the end of 1963, the business proved unsustainable—or at least unable to support our family. Dad found a job with Weaver Brothers trucking company, and we moved back to Spenard, into a brand-new three-bedroom house over an unfinished basement. Dad framed a few walls in the basement to form an office and a bedroom, and they continued Freight Service Company on the side, with the clackety mimeograph machine.

Our new house brought a big improvement to our living situation, but I missed my old friends. The Beatles appeared on "The Ed Sullivan Show" in February, a few weeks after we moved, and I wanted to know what my old friends thought of them. But I lacked the social confidence to pick up the phone and call.

Three months after our move to Spenard, the earthquake hit, and everything changed. From survival to recovery to rebuilding, the transportation industries in Alaska filled critical roles, and both Dad and Mom pitched in with everyone else. Intense work schedules exacted a toll on family life, and alcohol took the edge off for Dad.

In the year between the earthquake and our departure on the Drive, Dad often worked on the Kenai Peninsula, two or three hours south of Anchorage, depending on the tide schedule. He consumed coffee for breakfast, burgers and beer for lunch and dinner at roadside diners, and more beer to relax at night.

When we drove out of Anchorage in May 1965, Dad spent three-and-a-half months on his own. He kept up the same work schedule, but with no family pressures, no fights with Mom, and nobody to coax him away from another drink.

Mom's letters home, written almost daily that summer, repeat the refrain "sure hope there's a letter from you" at the next stop. He did write a few times— there are seven letters from him over our fourteen weeks of travel—but never enough to fill her need.

Long distance calls cost far too much to keep in touch that way. On a postcard the day we headed to

Canada on our return trip, Mom wrote *"Hope you got the message from S/L [SeaLand] Seattle."* At that late date, she had no more expectations of news from him. We would be home in a week—but did he even look forward to our return? I don't know, and I'm not sure she knew either.

I do know this: after the Drive, arguments grew louder and longer. One evening as they drank from round lowball glasses, their voices rose. I could hear them from my bedroom, and I wandered into the hall in time to see Mom throw her glass, smashing it against the dinette table in the kitchen. The crash of that broken glass awakened me to the seriousness of their collapsing relationship. The scratches in the Formica tabletop provided a constant reminder.

I hid from the noise of battle, wielding a flashlight on my homework or a book, and curling up on the floor of my bedroom closet with the door shut. In 1966 I began ninth grade at yet another school; Romig Junior High finally opened, a twenty-five-minute walk from home. That winter Mom became pregnant, and when spring arrived Dad announced his transfer from Anchorage to North Kenai, about four hours south by road, to manage a trucking terminal for Weaver Brothers. The company would place a modular house on their property where our family could live.

Marlie and I wept. We planned to attend West Anchorage High, the coolest school in town, where Jim was finishing his sophomore year. Kenai was nowhere—how could we live there, with none of our friends? One of our uncles had lived in Kenai years earlier, and we remembered it as a backwater.

With the baby due in July, Mom planned to stay in Anchorage for the birth. Dad moved to North Kenai and his new post in the spring, but Marlie, Glenn, and I stayed in Anchorage with Mom, savoring our final weeks in the city.

Marlie finished seventh grade that spring. Mikie slept over at our house one night, and they sneaked a boy into the basement through a window. Despite their foolproof plan, the boy's muddy footprints on top of the washing machine gave them away. Mom banished Marlie, over her wails of protest, to spend the summer in Kenai with Dad.

Three days after Marlie left, Mom called to see how she was doing, and how Dad was doing with her. "What did you have for dinner?"

"A hamburger."

"Did Dad take you out somewhere?"

"We went to the Hunger Hut."

Mom recognized the name of a local tavern Dad had mentioned, less than a mile from the freight terminal where our new modular home sat.

"What about lunch?"

"Dad sent me up to the Hunger Hut to bring back hamburgers."

"Sounds like you're eating a lot of burgers."

"Yeah. Every meal."

"What about breakfast?"

"We had hamburgers for breakfast too."

She'd been with Dad three days and ate nine hamburgers at the local tavern full of truck drivers and construction workers. She found a job babysitting a little boy whose mother was a prostitute.

Mom faltered in her confidence that Marlie might learn the intended lesson from her exile on Kenai's North Road. The area experienced a construction boom that brought oilfield workers and transient roustabouts from the oil patches around Texas and Oklahoma. While government and business leaders hailed the economic opportunities, a rough living and hard drinking population moved into trailer parks that sprung up overnight along Kenai's North Road.

More arguments ensued between Mom and Dad, by phone this time. Once again, Mom's absence left Dad free to live as he liked, drinking as many meals as he ate. Marlie survived the neglect and reveled in her freedom that summer.

In early August, Mom gave birth to our baby sister, Dyana, and we all joined Dad in Kenai. He spent little time with his family; he managed the trucking terminal and drank. Mom suffered health complications over the next eighteen months, and spent Thanksgiving one year in the Anchorage hospital. That year we ate Thanksgiving dinner at one of Dad's routine watering holes, a place heavy on the bar and light on the restaurant.

Mom was by no means a teetotaler, and in the spirit of "if you can't beat 'em, join 'em" she often joined Dad. Unfortunately, alcohol often left her sick. When they returned from a night out, Dad usually passed out but Mom threw up.

In January of my junior year of high school, I traveled to New Zealand for a year-long student exchange. That summer while I lived ten thousand miles away, Mom and Phyllis cooked up another grand plan, building a cabin on a lot they owned in Moose Pass. This provided my parents another separation, space apart and relief from their increasingly toxic relationship.

Phyllis named the cabin Mogmog, after a South Pacific island paradise in Micronesia, about halfway between Guam and Palau, where palm trees swayed in the warm breeze and the ocean's bounty teemed just beyond the island's fringe of sand. Phyl and Mom waxed lyrical about such places, dreamy-eyed as they spoke of living off the land, feasting on tropical fruits and seafood. No alarm clocks dragged a person from sleep to prepare for a mundane job. A beautiful escape from the world's rat race. They imagined their own Mogmog, the cabin in Moose Pass, would provide an escape for them, minus the palm trees.

Letters and photos from home reached me in New Zealand, telling of their progress building Mogmog. When I returned in mid-December 1969, I learned that Dad had transferred to another position with the trucking company and moved back to Anchorage months earlier.

Mom rented an apartment in Kenai, where we lived until I finished high school in May. Mom knew I stood a chance at a college scholarship at Kenai Central High and didn't want to jeopardize that by transferring me to another school before graduation. Another separation and another period of relative peace at home because of it.

By this time, Marlie and I formed many friendships in Kenai, and appreciated the benefits of a smaller community and high school. The move to Kenai gave us opportunities we wouldn't have had in Anchorage.

The summer of 1970, after graduation, I worked in a salmon cannery in Chignik on the remote Alaska Peninsula, along with ten of my high school classmates. Cannery work can be lucrative in a good fishing season, and a great way to save money, especially in a tiny remote village like Chignik, with no place to spend it.

Late that summer, Mom rejoined Dad in Anchorage, and I hitched a ride with a cousin from

Moose Pass, to start school at the University of Alaska, Fairbanks, almost four hundred miles away, taking advantage of my academic scholarship.

Marlie stayed in Kenai and married her high school beau. Glenn wanted desperately to play basketball in high school, so Mom arranged for him to live with her brother's family in Chugiak, and attend a smaller high school, about twenty-five miles north of Anchorage. Our uncle coached basketball there, so Glenn received good coaching and a position on the team.

In the three months between May and September of 1970, Marlie, Glenn, and I all left home one way or another. Mom had only our three-year-old sister, Dyana, living with her and Dad.

Within another few months, my parents separated permanently.

The Drive in '65 did not create the wedge that divided my parents. They were mismatched from the beginning, although they enjoyed a decade of fairly harmonious marriage. I think the summer of 1965 gave my father time to recognize and acknowledge to himself how unhappy he was. He handled that knowledge poorly, and Mom's desperation to keep the marriage together didn't help. That summer of adventure, separating my parents for fourteen weeks, started the ball rolling toward their inevitable divorce.

In the spring of 1973, both Mom and Dad began second marriages. Through some surreal alignment of events, both their weddings—held six weeks apart—involved the same minister and identical marriage ceremonies. Both hoped for happier relationships, and I certainly wished them well.

Chapter 27

IN THE FALL OF 1960, John Steinbeck prepared to leave his Sag Harbor home "in search of America," the subtitle he gave his subsequent book, *Travels with Charley*. Hurricane Donna delayed his planned Labor Day departure, roaring up the coast toward Long Island packing a wallop. Steinbeck nearly drowned after venturing outside to save his boat. Homes lost power, trees toppled, houses on lower ground flooded to the second floor, and his home on high ground was knocked about by the blast. But his truck and camper, custom-fitted for his journey, remained unscathed, just as our Wayward Bus survived the earthquake in 1964.

"Many a trip continues long after movement in time and space have ceased," Steinbeck wrote near the end of his account of that journey. For us, that was certainly true: The Drive in '65 lived on in ways large and small. In my love of maps, and the nostalgia generated by the whine of tires on a highway. My greater sense of history, and connections to a widespread family. And always, the longing to see more of the big wide world.

Our transformational summer did not bring immediate changes, nothing obvious to the casual observer. But we all changed. We had achieved what people doubted we could do, something brave and risky and inspiring. Our closer friends gazed in wonder as we related tales of the great beyond, the world outside Alaska. Our cousins listened with awe and envy.

My awareness of a wider world expanded beyond North America. We survived the Drive, and anything was possible. Within four years of our return, in January 1969, at sixteen years old, I left Alaska for a year of school at the opposite end of the world, in New Zealand. Mom flew with me to Seattle and put me on a ship in Vancouver, Canada. I arrived in Auckland ten days later and traveled to a small town on the South Island, hub of an agricultural area, a completely different life from Alaska. For eleven months, I wore uniforms to school, learned to play tennis, crafted clothes on a treadle sewing machine, and became part of another family with connections that remain strong fifty years later. The sense of adventure instilled in me on the Drive gave me a wanderlust that continues to urge me on to new places.

I wasn't the only one. After the birth of my sister Dyana in 1967, Mom began a career as a travel agent. She worked for travel agencies and airlines over the next several years, finally owning Billiken Travel, a successful agency in downtown Seattle's iconic Smith Tower. When China opened its borders to tourism in the 1980s, Mom joined the first group of travel agents to visit on a month-long familiarization tour. China had little tourism experience or infrastructure, so her group carried their own bags—before wheeled suitcases were developed. Mom suffered a painful strain in her arm. She agreed to acupuncture treatment, administered by an elderly man with foot-long needles, a remedy that relieved her pain completely. She organized tours to Mexico, accompanied groups on cruises, and enjoyed personal travel to Europe, Asia, New Zealand, and Australia, and through the United States.

Mom and Phyllis continued to inspire, and join in, other adventures with me. Phyllis and I shared the same favorite English professor in Anchorage in the early 1970's, and about twenty years later we attended the Oregon Shakespeare Festival together—something I had dreamed of since those college days.

Phyllis hosted family reunions every five years—lavish weekend affairs for more than a hundred people, events that she and Mom spent months planning. The tradition continues today, with a third generation of party planners now trying to live up to Phyllis's panache.

When their brother Don was mining gold near Alaska's border with the Yukon Territory, I drove up to the mine, more than nine hours northeast of Anchorage, with Mom, Phyllis, and my sister Dyana. We joined in a sing-along at Action Jackson's, the local watering hole, with Uncle Don and my cousins. I'd never seen landscape like the enormous mounding hills of that area south of the Yukon River, wild country that drew gold-seekers more than a hundred years ago.

In May of 1992, six months after the Soviet Union collapsed, Mom and I joined Glenn with a group of business and cultural leaders for several days in Petropavlovsk-Kamchatski, a military city in the

Russian Far East.

Travel influenced us all. Jim, of course, flew to Vietnam under government sponsorship in the uniform of the U.S. Air Force. As post-military jobs developed into a career, the path he chose was truck driving, specializing in oversized loads. A road trip every day.

Mikie bummed around Europe with a friend for a few months after high school, and in her early twenties she opened a travel agency. Later she worked for an airline. Mikie loved taking advantage of the travel benefits offered by her career. She returned to Europe, explored Africa on a photo safari, and visited New Zealand and Australia.

Phyllis invited Gram to visit Europe with her a few years after the Drive, but Gram needed a passport. That required a birth certificate, which she didn't have, and the State of New York would not provide a certificate for her unregistered birth. One of her brothers swore out an affidavit attesting to her birth, which allowed her to obtain the passport for the trip.

Phyllis loved road trips, and snapped photos wherever she and Bill traveled. Her photo albums filled ten or twelve boxes when she moved into assisted living in 2007. Most of these photos were cross-country shots, unlabeled as to date or location, but reminding her of places she had been. She explored the shapes in rock formations, seeking out the profiles of battleships or panting dogs, the way some people find images in clouds. Rocky ledges and promontories figured heavily among her photos.

Marlie worked most of her career for small plane flying services and a remote lodge in Alaska, living in our home state long after the rest of our family moved away. But she traveled the world as well. She's been to a few Olympic Games, ziplined in Roatán with her son and his wife, and set foot on every continent but Antarctica. Together, Marlie and I traveled to England, Italy, and several parts of the U.S. researching our family history.

I asked Glenn about the influence of the Drive in his life. "I think about it often," he said. "Like when I'm in the eighth hour on the fourth day of a road trip in the steaming heat with my clothes sticky and sticking to the seat and my back hurting and wondering how this seemed like a good enough idea to spend four months planning it, when all I really needed was a week in a quiet place with a hot tub and peace and quiet. Then, six months later, I repeat the experience."

Glenn surpassed us all in adventuresome travel, and he's passing the dream along. He climbed the peak above Machu Picchu with two of my children, took his daughter to the Ice Festival in Harbin, China, and visited Scotland with another niece and her husband in his ongoing quest to visit every whisky distillery in that country.

He can't decide which was his most adventurous: An icebreaker trip in the Russian Arctic, transferring at sea between two nuclear-powered ships by riding in a cage suspended by a crane, and finally arriving in Murmansk during a storm that killed more than twenty people, or perhaps a visit to Russia's Komandorski Islands with an Alaskan Aleut friend for a ceremony to rebury the remains of the explorer Vitus Bering, followed by a few days hiking the west coast of the Kamchatka Peninsula, where his friends and their guides caught cherry salmon, the southernmost Pacific salmon, found in the western ocean off Korea, Japan, and Kamchatka. While eating the salmon for dinner, they listened to one guide's father play a squeeze box and sing Russian folk songs by the river all evening.

For his next adventure, Glenn is considering a visit to Mongolia, or perhaps a float trip from Lake Baikal to the Arctic Ocean, a two- to four-month journey.

These days I often travel to family history locations, whether in the U.S. or points beyond. Marlie and I make such a trip together every two or three years. We found the graves of great-great-grandparents in a tiny Idaho community where an elderly lady shared her childhood memories of them teasing each other as they drove past in their wagon. In a Staffordshire, England, village, we paused by the creek where another distant grandparent drowned, a widow who spent twenty years in the local poorhouse. We gazed at the empty windows of the Palazzo Gualtieri in a town in the toe of Italy, questioning the truth of a tale told by a distant cousin: Did an ancestor really lose this four-story house on a gambling bet?

And I still love a road trip, when time allows. The freedom to stop and read every historical marker I see—that means a lot to me. Whether exploring backroads, wondering what's around the next bend, or cruising the interstate with my feet on the dash as I read aloud to my husband, I embrace a sense of curiosity about whatever is up ahead. The shared adventure of the Drive kept reminding all of us that the world is full of unexpected curiosities, with always something new to discover. I have a profound gratitude to Mom and Phyllis for launching me into such a life.

Both Dad and Uncle Bill died a few weeks apart in 2001. But Dad had changed since he and Mom divorced. He remarried and moved to Oregon, and for several years continued drinking heavily. After a health crisis about 1985, he finally sought help and quit drinking. I am forever grateful that my own children knew him and his second family during those sober years.

At seventy-five, Gram still jumped on a trampoline with her grandchildren and great-grandchildren. She died at the venerable age of ninety-six, in January 2004, having spent much of her nearly fifty-year widowhood as a beloved household member with one or another of her children.

Around the year 2000, Mikie was diagnosed with non-Hodgkin's lymphoma. She and her husband adopted two little boys not long before, and she used every weapon in the medical arsenal to fight the disease. A bone marrow transplant and other treatments compromised her immune system, and in 2005 an infection proved fatal. She had recently turned fifty-one.

At that time, Phyllis lived in the same small town in Eastern Washington where Mikie's family lived, and her changing behavior, especially since Uncle Bill's death in 2001, caused us all some concern. An excellent cook and creative hostess, for years Phyllis prepared sourdough pancake breakfast on Sundays with a standing open house invitation to any who wanted to stop by. One Sunday morning she called Mom, nearly in tears, to ask, "How do you make sourdough pancakes?"

After Mikie's death, Phyl's anxiety and disorientation increased. She began calling Mikie's husband in a panic because she had misplaced her keys or purse, or became convinced someone had stolen her jewelry. Mishaps with her car raised further red flags, and more than once she lost her way driving in the town of four hundred people where she had lived for fifteen years.

Her son, Jim, battled liver cancer, and by 2007 he wasn't expected to live long. Mikie's husband was overwhelmed with his circumstances as a single dad, and Phyllis's needs became too great for him to address. Jim and his family couldn't help Phyllis. Mom and I traveled to visit her a couple of times in early 2007, along with my cousin Suzan. We all recognized that Phyllis suffered from dementia, but she was adamant that she remain in her home.

Finally, I convinced her to stay for a while near Mom and I, because we lived nearer to Jim and could take her to visit him. When she railed against the concerns for her competence, I suggested she be tested by specialists in Seattle to reassure everyone.

We moved her about six weeks before Jim died, and she visited with him a few times and attended his memorial service. By then, specialists confirmed a diagnosis of Alzheimer's disease, and I offered to serve as her legal guardian. She lived in assisted living, less than a mile from me.

Mom and I visited often, picked berries with her, and treated her to hazelnut lattes, her favorite. I accompanied her to church for several months, until one Sunday, about ten minutes into the sermon, she leaned toward me with a disgusted look and asked, in a voice that could be heard three rows away, "Is this guy ever going to shut up?"

On one outing, a couple of years after moving, she and Mom talked about Jim, sharing their sadness over his death. Phyllis paused, a frown reflecting her mental struggle. Finally she spoke. "Wasn't there also a little girl?"

"Yes," Mom assured her, barely able to talk for the lump in her throat. "Her name was Mikie."

Phyllis loved to sing and possessed a beautiful voice. Even when the memories of her family faded to a blank canvas, and news of the extended family meant nothing to her, we could sing together, her music memory intact. She passed away in August 2013.

Mom began to write about her childhood and her family's move from Long Island to Moose Pass in 1945, but her health was fragile. I encouraged her, even as she moved to a retirement home at the age of eighty.

At that time I started writing about the Drive in '65 in earnest, eager to capture Mom's memories. I accompanied her to many doctor appointments, and read bits and pieces to her in waiting rooms. I described to her the photos I'd found, because by this time macular degeneration rendered Mom legally blind. She'd endured lung cancer, open heart surgery, eight stents, kidney failure, non-Hodgkin's lymphoma, and a number of less serious ailments. The clock was ticking. Loudly.

Then the ticking stopped. Faster than speed-dial, with a morning phone call from a caregiver, I learned that she passed away in the early morning hours of September 6, 2017, with no dramatic medical event or tender words we might know were final.

The mom who taught me to dream big and take risks was gone, on to the adventures of the next life, and I wrote alone, calling Marlie and Glenn for their recollections, wondering what Mom would have said about our visit to Seattle in 1965, or the last long stretch of road from Haines to Anchorage.

A few weeks later, as Marlie and I sorted through boxes from Mom's apartment, we found another trove of letters and keepsakes from the Drive, Mom's last gift. With that, I could finish this story.

Author's Note

Some readers may reasonably ask how I could recall so many details more than fifty years after the events of this book. Again, I credit Mom and Phyllis for their foresight in insisting that all our letters be saved. However, their collection of Drive archives extends far beyond the letters.

Maps and travel brochures fill a briefcase. Ticket stubs and gas receipts, highway guidebooks and business cards contribute names and details. Phyllis's small black ledger book contains notes from our earliest planning, and detailed expenses documented for most of the trip. Mom's personal diary, and even the envelopes from our correspondence with their postmarks confirming many dates and places, made it possible to recreate the journey.

I have all the photographs from the trip, from our departure photo on the front cover of this book, to the last photo of the Wayward Bus coming off the ferry in Haines, ready for those last grueling seven hundred and fifty miles. I considered including some photos in this book, but the photo quality left me doubtful of their value in black and white reproduction. However, I will share them on my author website—I hope you will visit to see them. **I'll welcome you warmly with a free story of old Moose Pass, when you sign up for my occasional newsletters at www.SandraLynneReed.com.**

CPSIA information can be obtained
at www.ICGtesting.com
Printed in the USA
LVHW042014010820
662075LV00003B/215